The Identity Security Imperative

A Leader's Guide to Securing Every Identity

A Security Matters Publication
by CyberArk

CYBEREDGE
PRESS™

The Identity Security Imperative
A Leader's Guide to Securing Every Identity

Published by:
CyberEdge Group, LLC
501 E. Las Olas Boulevard
Suite 300
Fort Lauderdale, FL 33301
(800) 327-8711
www.cyberedgegroup.com

For general information on CyberEdge Group research and marketing consulting services, or to create a custom book and eBook for your organization, contact our sales department at 800-327-8711 or info@cyberedgegroup.com.

ISBN: 978-1-948939-45-4 (Paperback)
ISBN: 978-1-948939-46-1 (eBook)

Printed in the United States of America.

10 9 8 7 6 5 4 3 2 1

Table of Contents

Foreword v

Why Security Leaders Should Read This Book vii

I. Understanding Identity Security

Chapter 1: Identity Security: The Paradigm Shift 3

Chapter 2: What Is Identity Security? 19

Chapter 3: How Identity Security Fits into Enterprise Security Programs 25

Chapter 4: Critical Capabilities for an Identity Security Platform 33

Chapter 5: Overview of Intelligent Privilege Controls™ 37

II. Securing the Full Spectrum of Identities

Chapter 6: Understanding Identity-related Risk 49

Chapter 7: Workforce Identities 55

Chapter 8: IT User Identities 59

Chapter 9: Developer Identities 63

Chapter 10: Machine Identities 69

III. Implementing an Identity Security Program

Chapter 11: How Identity Security Enables Zero Trust 77

Chapter 12: Cybersecurity Frameworks, Regulations, and Insurance 79

Chapter 13: Developing Your Identity Security Program 85

Chapter 14: Case Studies 99

IV. Navigating the Future

Chapter 15: The Power of AI 109

Chapter 16: LLMs Require Extra Caution 117

Chapter 17: Quantum Readiness 119

Conclusion 125

Foreword

Workforce users, IT users, developers, machines. Digital identities are the pulse of an organization. They're how we share and access information across networks, collaborate with supply chains, and get work done. And identities are also the gateway to an organization's sensitive information and most valuable assets.

Unfortunately, attackers know this. That's why 93% of organizations have experienced identity-related cyberattacks over the past year. When an identity is compromised and sensitive data falls into the wrong hands, it puts all of us at risk. It can harm our livelihoods, our colleagues, and the trust we put in organizations.

Today's attacks aren't just isolated breaches by lone actors. They are coordinated, relentless, and more advanced than ever. The proliferation of human and machine identities, the emergence of new IT environments, and new attacks using generative AI are exposing gaps in our traditional defenses.

In fact, AI itself needs to be secure. With agents, bots, and custom GPTs already augmenting human work, AI is creating a new class of machine identities that will need to be secured, along with the AI processes producing them.

This critical moment demands a paradigm shift in how we secure and defend our identities and, by extension, our organizations. It's no longer enough to just manage identities. We must embrace identity security, and we must act quickly.

To enable this paradigm shift, I believe we need intelligent identity security solutions that include dynamic, just-in-time access and zero standing privileges so users can work the way they need to. We need proactive defenses that empower security teams to prevent, detect, and respond to evolving threats in real time. AI shouldn't just be a tool for attackers; it should also give defenders the advantage of more effective insights and data so they can contain incidents before they can cause harm.

We wrote this book for everyone invested in cybersecurity—CISOs, practitioners, and anyone else who is passionate about building a secure digital future. The private sector can and must lead the charge to drive identity security forward. We cannot wait for regulations to catch up; we delay at our peril. Business resilience begins with securing identities today and laying the foundation for tomorrow's defense. Together, we can prepare for what lies ahead by focusing on the needs of our workforce and integrating identity security at every level of our operations.

We thank everyone who helped make this book possible, including our customers, industry experts, and the CyberArk team. We're on a shared mission: to secure the world against cyber threats, so together we can move fearlessly forward. We believe this mission starts with securing every identity.

Matt Cohen
CEO
CyberArk

Why Security Leaders Should Read This Book

I f you're a Chief Information Security Officer, your role is more critical—and complex—than ever. The stakes are high: cyber threats evolve at breakneck speed, regulatory pressures mount, AI is top of mind for digital transformation, and demands for operational efficiency are relentless. Your mandate is to protect your organization's digital crown jewels while enabling the business to innovate and grow securely.

This book was written with you in mind. It provides a comprehensive guide for tackling your most pressing challenges and achieving your strategic objectives.

If you're a member of the extended security leadership team, this book is for you as well. As a day-to-day leader and planner, you enable the various pillars of identity security to operate. As you read this book, we encourage you to think about how its concepts apply in your security domain.

A new paradigm for identity security

Identity is at the heart of your cybersecurity strategy. However, traditional approaches are no longer sufficient. This book introduces a forward-thinking framework that helps you leverage the key concepts of identity security and elevates the discipline of securing identities into a cornerstone of your defense strategy. By considering a consolidated approach to protecting digital identities with the right level of privilege controls, you'll strengthen business resilience, gain the upper hand against sophisticated threats, and reduce your organization's risk exposure.

Take top challenges head-on

We understand your pain points:

- ☑ **Protecting mission-critical services from ransomware and improving cyber resilience** are essential for business continuity. You need actionable strategies to build strong defenses and recovery plans.

- ☑ **Communicating risk and compliance metrics to the board** is crucial to securing buy-in and funding. Here, you'll find tools to frame these conversations in a way that resonates with business leaders.

- ☑ **Talent shortages and burnout** in cybersecurity are real and growing concerns. Learn how to optimize your team's workload through automation and process improvements while fostering a culture of resilience and growth.

- ☑ **Meeting regulatory and audit requirements** can be daunting. This book simplifies the path to compliance and aligns your efforts with industry standards and legal mandates.

- ☑ **Implementing cybersecurity framework best practices** for identities ensures your security posture evolves alongside emerging threats. We break down how to operationalize these practices effectively.

Solve complex challenges with practical solutions

In the chapters that follow, we'll show you how to:

- ☑ **Respond to threats faster** through advanced detection and response capabilities

- ☑ **Operationalize zero trust architecture** to secure your organization from the inside out

- ☑ **Strengthen cloud and SaaS security** to safeguard your expanding digital ecosystem

- ☑ **Optimize controls for cyber insurance** to reduce premium costs and improve policy terms

☑ **Enhance the user experience** by streamlining secure access to enterprise resources and balancing security with usability

☑ **Integrate secrets management into the SSDLC** to protect your software supply chain

☑ **Automate IAM processes** to improve efficiency, reduce errors, and lower total cost of ownership (TCO)

Align cybersecurity with business goals

Success in cyber defense is about more than just mitigating risks. Leaders must improve operational efficiency, ensure compliance, and drive secure digital transformation. We'll show you how to align all these goals to drive meaningful outcomes that elevate your role as a business enabler.

Achieve your OKRs with confidence

Whether your objectives and key results include speeding up detection and response times, maturing your zero trust initiatives, tightening up compliance readiness—or all the above—this book provides frameworks, insights, and tools to help you succeed. More importantly, it can help you demonstrate clear, measurable progress to your stakeholders.

The future of identity security is already here. Forward-thinking CISOs who embrace collaboration across their organization and carefully steer AI-enabled transformation can foster trust and achieve lasting success in whatever they are striving to build.

This book is your how-to guide.

Helpful Icons

Tips provide practical advice that you can apply in your own organization.

When you see this icon, take note as the related content contains key information that you won't want to forget.

Proceed with caution because if you don't it may prove costly to you and your organization.

Content associated with this icon is more technical in nature and is intended for IT practitioners.

Want to learn more? Follow the corresponding URL to discover additional content available on the Web.

I. Understanding Identity Security

Chapter 1

Identity Security: The Paradigm Shift

- Learn why organizations need a new paradigm for securing identities
- Review changes and new challenges that are making existing practices obsolete
- Discover a new approach to identity security that meets these challenges

A New Paradigm Is Needed

Cybersecurity identities are the foundational elements upon which organizational access and data security rest. Yet the stark reality is that most organizations are relying on defenses designed for last year's cyberattacks and an outmoded model for controlling access to critical applications, data, and infrastructure.

In fact, there is an ever-widening gap between the threats to identities and access control and our ability to defend against those threats. If we continue to do things the same way we do now, the gap will widen, and we will fall farther and farther behind (see Figure 1-1).

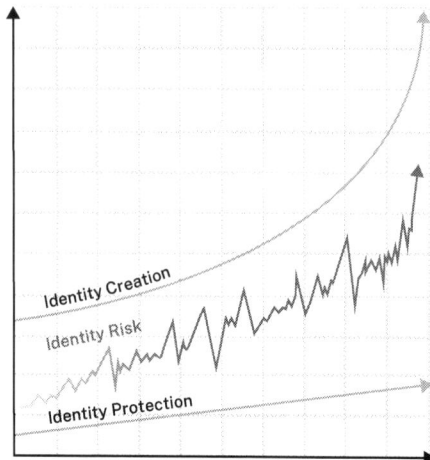

Figure 1-1: The explosive growth in identities is parabolic while the ability to protect identities falls further behind, creating a widening gap to defend against threats.

Our existing paradigm for employing identities to control access is outmoded because, among other shortcomings, it:

- ☑ Doesn't address new groups of identities (including "machine" or "non-human" identities)
- ☑ Isn't adapted for cloud environments
- ☑ Can't scale to handle the exploding volume of identities that threat actors can target
- ☑ Operates in information and workflow silos
- ☑ Lacks security capabilities needed to detect and respond to today's sophisticated threats

Let's examine the technology and business developments that are widening the gulf between identity-related threats and defenses. Then we'll introduce a new way of thinking about cybersecurity identities that will help organizations eliminate the gap.

ON THE WEB How important are compromised identities and credentials for cybercriminals? Thirty-one percent of breaches in the past 10 years involved stolen credentials, and compromised credentials are a more common data breach strategy than either phishing or exploiting vulnerabilities ("Verizon 2024 Data Breach Investigation Report" https://www.verizon.com/business/resources/reports/dbir/). Ninety-three percent of organizations faced two or more identity-related breaches in the past year ("The CyberArk 2024 Identity Security Threat Landscape Report" https://www.cyberark.com/resources/ebooks/identity-security-threat-landscape-2024-report).

What Worked Before Isn't Working Now

Let's examine why most organizations are struggling to protect identities and ensure secure access to applications, data, and infrastructure.

More identity groups

In the past, most security teams treated all users more or less the same. They made a distinction between "privileged users," such as top executives and IT administrators who access highly confidential data and critical IT resources, and everyone else, but that was mostly a matter of applying more monitoring and security controls to the former and fewer to the latter.

Today, there are four major categories of identities, including one extremely important category of non-human users such as workloads and IoT devices (Figure 1-2). Each of the four categories—workforce users, IT users, developers, and machines—has its own set of risks and its own list of appropriate controls.

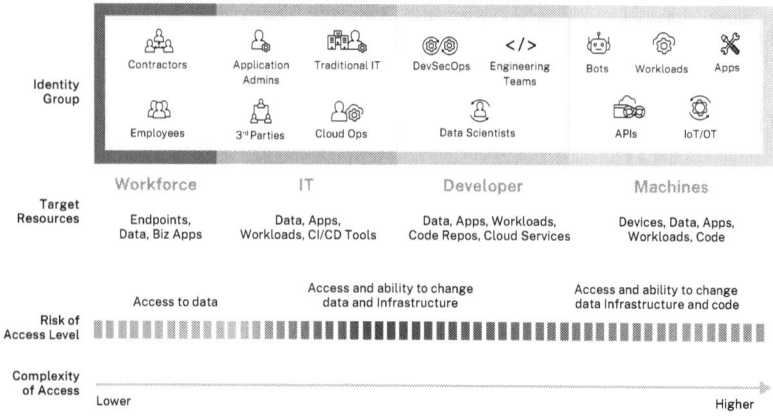

Figure 1-2: The four identity groups have different levels of identity-related risk associated with the spectrum of human and non-human identities.

Meet the Spectrum of Identities

Workforce users are employees and temporary contractors who engage with a variety of endpoints, SaaS applications, and data crucial for daily tasks.

IT users include traditional IT staff, third-party vendors, and cloud operations personnel who access a broad array of privileged environments such as SaaS applications and cloud platforms.

Developers include everyone from software development team members to DevSecOps staff to data scientists who perform AI/ML work in the cloud. Most need rapid access to admin roles and cloud-native services.

Machine identities (non-human users) encompass a mix of workloads, code, virtual machines (VMs), operational technology (OT) systems, and Internet of Things (IoT) devices that need to be protected from threat actors and other unauthorized users.

Each segment of these identities requires specific solutions that combine the capabilities of access management, privileged access management, identity governance and administration. Identity threat detection and response should be integrated in conjunction with these core capabilities as shown in Figure 1-3, on the next page.

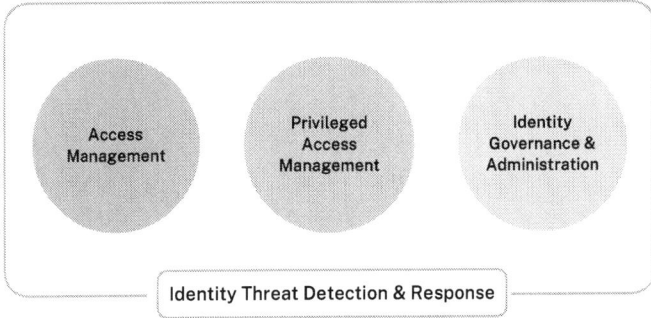

Figure 1-3: Each identity group requires a unique combination of identity management capabilities.

You'll learn more about these identity groups as you read the book. In Chapters 7 through 10, we'll explore the ways in which these identity group should be treated differently.

Surging populations of identities

Not only are there more distinct identity groups, the raw number of identities to be managed and protected is growing exponentially:

- ☑ As workforce users register for an increasing number of applications and cloud services, more and more identities are associated with each user.

- ☑ Software developer jobs in the United States are projected to grow by nearly 18% between 2023 and 2033 according to the U.S. Department of Labor, and most developers access and create multiple machine identities in different development environments on multiple cloud platforms.

- ☑ The number of machine identities continues to increase with the widespread adoption of cloud, containerized architectures such as Kubernetes and the use of DevOps and CI/CD tools. In fact, machine identities represent the fastest-growing category, outpacing human identity growth 45-to-1.

These exploding identity populations significantly expand the attack surface. Each device connected to the internet represents a potential entry point for malicious activities, including everything from privacy breaches and compliance issues to commandeering of devices.

Although non-human identities have become one of the riskiest identity groups, the CyberArk 2024 Identity Security Threat Landscape Report found that nearly two-thirds of organizations fail to recognize them as privileged users. But the fact is, almost 50% of machine identities have access to sensitive data.

Blurred boundaries between privileged users and others

Once it seemed possible to divide a workforce into privileged users, whose identities required special monitoring and controls, and everyone else. But today, almost anyone—from an IT user, to a third-party vendor, to your average employee—can become privileged in some situations because they need to access sensitive data, have a valid reason to acquire elevated permissions, or play a critical role in an operational workflow.

Also, the lines between identity groups continue to blur: IT users act more like developers; developers perform more self-managed IT functions; and workforce users are being trusted and empowered to administer their own SaaS applications. This blurring is especially prevalent in cloud and hybrid environments, where it exposes organizations to increased security risks.

In addition, identity security teams must find ways to protect the identities of the army of third and fourth-party vendors that deliver various technological solutions and services, which have become indispensable to the way we work. The immensity of this challenge is illustrated by the fact that 59% of organizations say they would not be able to protect against an attack stemming from a successful compromise of a software supply chain provider.

Engineers Are Also Admins

Before the days of the cloud, it was relatively simple to draw a sharp line between admins and users. Admins were privileged users, entitled to deploy, configure and manage applications. Other members of the software development community did not need to perform these tasks, and so could be treated as ordinary (non-privileged) users.

But on today's cloud platforms, many types of users need access to and control over cloud services and wide swaths of cloud infrastructure, in effect turning them into de facto admins. Such users include:

- Software developers (employees and contractors)
- DevSecOps engineers
- Site reliability engineers
- Data scientists
- Third parties with outsourced responsibility for managing and monitoring applications

The fact that many identities need admin-type permissions to do their jobs means that threat actors who capture the credentials of those users have the potential to take control of critical applications. Today these identities need to be treated as privileged users when they are performing admin-type tasks.

Protection of machine identities

Machine identities refer to all the workloads, applications, devices, and other non-human identities across the enterprise.

Machine identities are particularly problematic for most cybersecurity groups. Besides being numerous and widely distributed, bots, workloads, and AI agents that access devices, data, apps, and infrastructure have different risk levels depending on their function and scope. They also require secrets and credentials to authenticate and authorize their access. In addition, most operational technology systems and IoT devices were not designed with security or identity management in mind.

Identities everywhere

Traditionally, security focused on protecting the borders of an organization's IT infrastructure using firewalls, intrusion detection systems, and other perimeter defenses. The prevailing mindset was that threats originated from the outside, and everything inside the perimeter was secure and trustworthy.

However, the rise of cloud computing and software as a service (SaaS) has blurred or dissolved these network boundaries. Organizations routinely use resources that are not housed within their own data centers and are accessed over the internet. Many organizations have a combination of on-premises, operational technology (OT), and public cloud environments.

In addition, more and more employees work remotely from various locations and devices.

The wild west: new attacks

Creative new identity-based attacks are becoming more common, with results that are often devastating.

In 2020, SolarWinds became a household name when hackers introduced malicious code into its Orion software update, which used compromised machine identities to distribute malware to over 18,000 customers.

A misconfigured identity provider (IdP) was partly to blame for the MGM breach, which cost the resort giant well over $100 million. Attackers used the vulnerability to pivot into MGM's infrastructure in the Okta tenant and gain highly privileged access to Microsoft Azure, which ultimately allowed the cloud-originated attack to reach MGM's brick-and-mortar operations. The attackers used generative AI (Gen AI) to voice phish (or 'vish') employees and help desk teams, steal credentials, and reset multi-factor authentication (MFA) settings.

After a slow but stealthy password spray attack, nation-state attacker Cozy Bear accessed a legacy, non-production test tenant account in Microsoft's environment. Overly permissive trust relationships between non-production and production environments allowed the attackers to escalate privileges and move laterally across systems all the way to executive emails.

The rise in more potent attacks is driven by both skilled and unskilled threat actors who are leveraging GenAI to exploit the expanding and complex digital ecosystem by targeting unsecured identities to infiltrate victim environments. Malicious attackers are also devising innovative new techniques to leverage polymorphic malware, steal session cookies, and find other ways to evade existing security controls.

The growing difficulty in detecting AI-powered cyberattacks has heightened the risk of widespread breaches.

The cloud

The cloud changed business forever. It's enabled organizations' rapid digital transformation by offering unlimited capabilities and resources for the workforce and streamlining operational efficiencies. However, cloud environments, and particularly cloud platforms such as Amazon Web Services (AWS), Microsoft Azure, and Google Cloud Platform (GCP), introduce a host of new complexities related to infrastructure, entitlements, and roles.

At one time, applications were monolithic and relied on only a few underlying shared services provided by an operating system on a particular piece of hardware. In those days, a relatively small set of entitlements could be used to control access to applications and system software.

Applications "lifted and shifted" onto cloud platforms are more complicated and operate in a vastly more complex environment. Typical cloud-hosted applications can be:

- ☑ Comprised of dozens of modular components

- ☑ Running in virtual machines and containers managed by hypervisors and container technologies like Kubernetes and Docker

- ☑ Interacting with a wide range of networking, storage, data management, deployment, and other shared runtime services

- ☑ Monitored and tuned by third-party operations management, orchestration and security tools

- ☑ Configured and managed with infrastructure software provided by cloud service providers (CSPs)

- ☑ Residing on several cloud platforms

Security leaders must set permissions for access and actions across dozens or hundreds of workloads and services just for one application. In fact, an analysis has shown that a single user might be able to access approximately 1,400 native cloud services that collectively have 40,000 different entitlements.

Also, a single action by one user might require multiple authorizations. For example, a developer observing an application component might need access to the cloud platform, then to a virtual machine (VM) where the component is running, and then to the component itself.

Yet another complication of cloud environments is that shared services and application workloads are constantly being spun up and taken down to adjust to changing demand. Identity security solutions must be able to detect and control access to these ephemeral resources.

The bottom line is that identity security teams must manage a staggeringly large number of entitlements.

OT systems and IoT devices

Securing operational technology (OT) environments and Internet of Things (IoT) devices is crucial for protecting critical infrastructure and sensitive data.

Historically, air-gapping, or network segmentation for OT environments and small devices with chips, was a best practice. However, with the convergence of IT and OT environments and the explosion in the number of IoT devices, this is no longer the case, and identity security needs to be extended to control access to OT systems and IoT devices. In fact, securing OT and IoT systems has become a matter of great urgency, since both private groups and nation-states are known to target cyber-physical systems because of the potentially devasting impact of disabling them.

Few OT systems and IoT devices were designed with security in mind. For example, many rely on simple user ID/password combinations for authentication (and are sometimes shipped with default passwords that have been published on the internet). Fundamental security functions like authentication, monitoring, and logging need to be implemented in front of them.

Some OT systems and IoT devices use secrets such as SSH keys, API and access keys, tokens, and certificates to authenticate themselves when accessing cloud environments, applications, data storage, and other cloud services. Unfortunately, often these secrets are not well protected, or not protected at all, from determined threat actors. Further, many organizations fail to enforce policies for creating, vaulting, and rotating secure credentials and keys.

SaaS applications

Many modern organizations are transitioning all their business applications to the cloud, barring a few required by regulations or compliance concerns to remain on-premises. Everything from human resource information systems (HRIS) to customer relationship management (CRM) solutions, enterprise resource planning (ERP), data management systems (DMS), payroll and financial management systems, and project management tools that were once hosted and maintained on-premises is likely to be a SaaS application.

The transition from on-premises business software to SaaS applications has been driven by factors such as lower upfront costs, scalability, automatic updates, accessibility for anyone with an internet connection, and easy integration with other systems through APIs.

However, along with these advantages, organizations need to consider SaaS drawbacks, such as a lack of visibility and challenges in collecting and correlating identity-related data across numerous SaaS applications. Businesses lose direct control, visibility, and insight over their data and infrastructure architecture because SaaS applications are managed by their providers. The consequences of these drawbacks make it challenging for organizations to respond to identity-related threats and attacks against their vendor-managed software.

Cloud-oriented enterprises typically rely on machine identities to secure and manage their cloud (and often their on-premises) environments. In the security area, this process typically involves cloud-based tools with wide access to cloud resources so they can scan for vulnerabilities, patch software, monitor user activities, and detect threats.

Unfortunately, we can see from the headlines that SaaS applications can be compromised by threat actors. For that reason, privileged users of many SaaS applications, including hosted security IT admin tools, need to be subject to close scrutiny of their entitlements and continuous monitoring of their actions.

A Paradigm Shift to Meet New Challenges

The aim of identity security is to ensure that the right individuals can access the right information resources at the right times for the right reasons. But as you can tell from the many changes and new challenges outlined in this chapter, the principles and methods that worked before aren't enough now.

A paradigm shift in identity security is underway to meet and overcome the new challenges. The major differences between the traditional paradigm and the new one fall into six areas (see Figure 1-4).

Traditional IAM	The New Paradigm
Designed for workforce identities	Designed for a spectrum of identities
Siloed identity management on-premises, in cloud platforms, and across SaaS applications.	Unified discovery, policy creation, and management across environments
Static, standing privileges	Adaptive and dynamic processes, zero standing privileges, just-in-time privileges based on context and risk
Commoditized access management (e.g., MFA and SSO)	Pre-and post-authentication protection (e.g., session isolation, secure browsing)
Focused on managing entitlements	Includes identity threat detection and response (ITDR)
	Embedded AI everywhere (admin, policy management, ITDR, etc.)

Figure 1-4: Differences between traditional IAM and the new identity security paradigm.

From workforce users to a spectrum of identities

In the past, identity management processes were designed for one important type of identity, the typical workforce user. Distinctions were made for privileged workforce users who might be covered by additional controls, but there was only one framework for providing controls and balancing risks with user requirements.

The new identity security paradigm posits that there is a spectrum of identities with significant differences in the roles, complexity of the environment, and risks. In particular, machine identities (which include software processes and agents as well as hardware devices) have management and security requirements fundamentally different from those appropriate to human identities.

From on-premises to unified multi-cloud, and SaaS

Many identity security tasks have been performed in silos. Today, unification is essential, including the unification of identity information discovery, policy creation and administration, and audits. It is also important that user experiences be consistent across all environments for all types of users.

Implementing these types of unification requires that identity security solutions be integrated with a wide range of applications and platforms and be able to work with the native tools in each.

From static to adaptive and dynamic

Today, security controls are mostly static, in the sense that once privileges are granted to identities their use for access control and authorization is fixed.

The new identity security paradigm is based on the idea that authentication and authorization need to be adaptive and continually adjusted. This is embodied in the principle of "zero standing privileges"; the idea that all standing entitlements should be removed from identities and privileges should be granted dynamically based on continual assessments of context and risk.

Dynamic processes are also critical for managing machine identities. Many types of software workloads and agents are continually being spun up and stood down in cloud VMs and cloud environments. Identity security systems must be able to assign and revoke appropriate privileges to those identities "just-in-time," at scale, with a high degree of automation.

Pre- and post-authentication protection

Identity security solutions have traditionally focused on a few extremely important areas of security such as advanced authentication and single sign-on (SSO).

But to meet new challenges from sophisticated threat actors, comprehensive identity security needs to expand to include additional technologies for pre- and post-authentication protection. These include:

- ☑ Session control
- ☑ Session isolation
- ☑ Secure browsing

These make it possible to require re-authentication during a high-risk web session to ensure that the person who initiated the session is the one using the application.

Expanding to include threat detection and response

The new paradigm extends the reach of identity security to include identity threat detection and response (ITDR). Because compromised identities and credentials are involved in so many attacks, identity security and security operations center (SOC) teams need to collect and analyze comprehensive identity-related information quickly and accurately to detect and contain threats.

Enhancing everything with AI

To keep up with new challenges, exploding volumes of identities and identity-related data, and the pace of change, identity security solution providers must embed AI capabilities across their product lines. This includes:

☑ Augmenting management tools with natural language capabilities so administrators and users can quickly and easily navigate tools, enter information, select parameters, and find guidance and direction.

☑ Providing features to enhance and streamline policy management, deployment, and optimization.

☑ Strengthen threat detection and response by detecting anomalies and recommending responses.

☑ Automating administration, detection, response, auditing, and planning processes of all kinds.

Details just ahead!

In the chapters ahead, we'll outline the basic characteristics of the new identity management paradigm as it relates to these six areas. We'll also explore the implications and show you how the new paradigm will help you:

☑ Differentiate and safeguard various types of administrative access

☑ Prevent identity compromise, privilege escalation, and lateral movement

☑ Integrate identity security with broader enterprise security strategies, including IAM, privileged access management (PAM), and endpoint security—without damaging the user experience

☑ Leverage zero standing privileges and AI-driven security solutions to close the gap between threat emergence and defense readiness

☑ Increase business resilience, boost productivity, and enable innovative new technology and business initiatives.

By the end of the book, you'll be able to lay out a strategic roadmap for implementing an identity security program.

Takeaways and recommendations

- The shift to cloud platforms introduces new challenges, including managing a vast number of entitlements and permissions that increase the attack surface.

- Today's cybercriminals leverage AI to increase the sophistication and scope of their attacks.

- The proliferation of identity groups, such as workforce users, IT users, developers, and machine identities has significantly expanded the attack surface.

- Organizations need to focus on securing both human and machine identities to protect their IT environments.

- A paradigm shift in identity security is underway to meet and overcome the new challenges.

Chapter 2

What Is Identity Security?

In this chapter

■ Understand the definition and scope of identity security

■ Appreciate why identity security is important

Identity Security Fundamentals

Identity security is the cybersecurity discipline concerned with reducing all aspects of identity-related risk. This discipline requires governing, identifying, and protecting all identities used within an organization, including those used to access applications, endpoints, infrastructure, and data stores. It also covers processes for detecting and responding to identity-related threats.

Identity security is built on lessons from the privileged access management (PAM) discipline founded by CyberArk 25 years ago. The notion that malicious actors concentrate on users with privileges isn't new, but the target identities, target environments, and attack methods are.

Implementing proactive and reactive identity security controls can mitigate the risks of identity compromise, lateral and vertical movement, and privilege escalation and abuse, and can break the attack chain that dominates information technology breaches. The same core principles that apply to PAM apply to all identities, which is why the general pattern of how threat actors compromise and exploit identities hasn't fundamentally changed. That identity attack chain is illustrated in Figure 2-1.

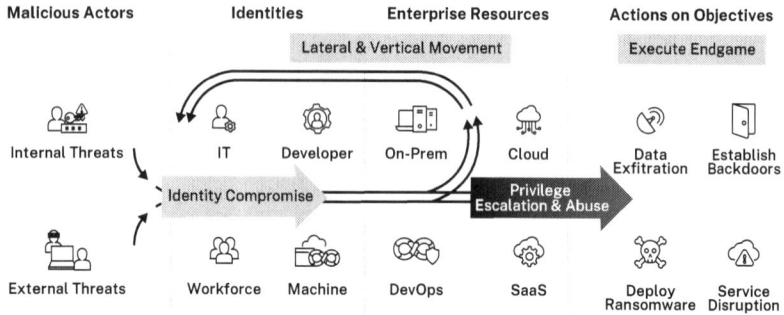

Figure 2-1: The identity attack chain.

PAM, the backbone of identity security

In the early days of computing, IT organizations stored passwords used to authenticate and authorize privileged users so they could manage sensitive assets. Privileged users held the keys to the IT kingdom, with the power to change, download, and delete confidential data, move money, configure systems and applications, and add and remove users.

However, organizations had only limited ability to track and control the activities of people with these powers. Privilege creep (users accumulating far more privileges than necessary for their jobs) was common. Privileged accounts often relied on default, shared, or weak passwords. When insiders intentionally or accidentally abused their rights, it was difficult to identify the culprits.

Twenty-five years ago, CyberArk delivered a solution to these issues: privileged access management. PAM is a comprehensive cybersecurity strategy for controlling, monitoring, securing, and auditing all privileged identities and their activities across an enterprise IT environment.

PAM features such as credential vaulting and rotation, password rotation, and session monitoring were initially deployed by highly regulated (and highly paranoid) organizations. However, over time, they were recognized as critical for all organizations.

Today, PAM forms the backbone of modern identity security and is high on every CISO's security checklist. But protecting identities and enterprise resources isn't a one-size-fits-all approach, which is why the discipline of identity security has evolved from the core concepts of PAM.

The complete scope of identity security includes:

1. **A spectrum of identities,** including workforce users, IT users, developers, third-party vendors, and machines (workloads, code, and applications)

2. **Resources,** including applications, endpoints, infrastructure, and data sources (some being particularly problematic, such as workforce and high-risk SaaS apps, cloud-native services, elastic cloud workloads and long-lived systems)

3. **Proactive controls,** including controls for authentication (validation that users are who they say they are), authorization (permissions and entitlements), access control (methods for protecting identities and restricting access to resources), and auditing (monitoring and logging how identities access and use resources)

4. **Reactive controls,** including controls for detecting and responding to identity-related threats, including detection of in-session malicious behavior and external signals of malicious activity

5. **Identity lifecycle management,** including managing how identities are created and administered and how access permissions are provisioned, certified, and de-provisioned

6. **Processes** needed to support all the business and technical workflows that operationalize identity lifecycle management and the management of identity security controls

As we mentioned in the last chapter, a comprehensive approach to identity security seeks to authenticate every identity accurately, authorize each identity with the proper permissions, and provide access for that identity to privileged assets in a structured manner—with auditing to ensure the entire process is sound.

This covers not only the four groups of identities we have been discussing, but also a very wide range of digital resources, as shown in Figure 2-2.

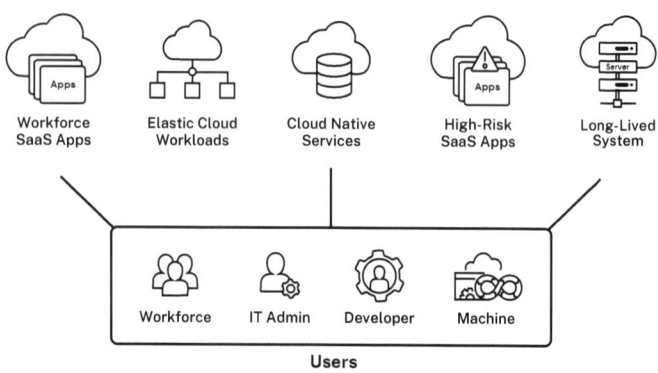

Figure 2-2: Today's identities and digital resources.

Implementing identity security requires a holistic approach centered on intelligent privilege controls, a topic we'll dive into in Chapter 5. Organizations can dynamically apply these security measures to protect an identity's access to any enterprise resource based on contextual factors like risk and user experience. This holistic approach seamlessly secures access to applications, infrastructure, and data by human and machine identities. It also enables organizations to flexibly automate the identity lifecycle.

What are intelligent privilege controls?

Intelligent privilege controls are identity security measures that can be dynamically applied to incoming requests for access and interaction with enterprise resources. We call them "intelligent" because their application can be modified in real time based on contextual factors such as the requester's level of authorization, the expected user experience, and the risk level of the task at hand.

You can learn more about intelligent privilege controls at: https://www.cyberark.com/what-is/intelligent-privilege-controls/

Why Identity Security Is Important

There's no shortage of reasons why identity security is important. Reducing cyber risk and improving your security posture to empower business resilience while also enabling accelerating digital transformation and business initiatives are key for security leaders to make an impact in the organization.

Identity security counters new attack types

Modern identity security frameworks employ dynamic and adaptive measures to monitor and secure identities, ensuring that only authorized users gain access to critical resources. By implementing intelligent privilege controls and continuous threat detection, organizations can mitigate risks associated with sophisticated phishing, deepfakes, and AI-powered malware attacks. Identity security can stop evolving cyber threats.

Identity security increases the effectiveness of security teams

By automating routine tasks and providing centralized visibility into all identities and access points, identity security enables security teams to focus on strategic initiatives and avoid being bogged down by manual access management tasks. Continuous monitoring and real-time threat detection permit quicker responses to potential threats, reduce the burden on cybersecurity personnel and increase overall operational efficiency.

Identity security enables new technologies and business initiatives

Identity security provides secure and seamless access across diverse environments. As organizations continue to adopt cloud services, remote work, and IoT devices, identity security ensures that all identities—human and machine—are properly authenticated and authorized. This strengthening of secure access enables digital transformation efforts, supports hybrid and multi-cloud environments, and facilitates the adoption of new services. By balancing robust security measures with low-friction user experiences, identity security helps drive innovation and business growth.

ON THE WEB

Learn more about identity security at
https://www.cyberark.com/identity-security/

Takeaways and recommendations

- PAM is a foundational layer of modern cybersecurity that involves controlling, monitoring, securing and auditing privileged identities.

- Identity security builds on the principles of PAM to strengthen governance and protection for both human and machine identities across diverse IT environments.

- Modern identity security frameworks employ dynamic controls to monitor and secure identities, mitigating risks from advanced cyber threats like phishing, deepfakes, and AI-powered attacks.

- Identity security enables secure adoption of new technologies, supports digital transformation and hybrid environments, and helps drive business growth by ensuring seamless and secure access for all identities.

Chapter 3

How Identity Security Fits into Enterprise Security Programs

In this chapter

- See how identity security contributes to key enterprise security domains
- Examine the pros and cons of making identity security a freestanding or notional program
- Familiarize yourself with eight qualities of successful identity security programs

Identity Security Contributes to Many Security Domains

Enterprise information security groups are typically organized into a number of programs responsible for different cybersecurity domains.

Identity security makes important contributions to many of those domains, including identity and access management (IAM), PAM, endpoint security, application security (AppSec), and SOC teams responsible for threat detection and response (TDR), governance, risk, and compliance (GRC), vulnerability management, data loss prevention (DLP), data privacy, network security, and business continuity and disaster recovery (BCDR).

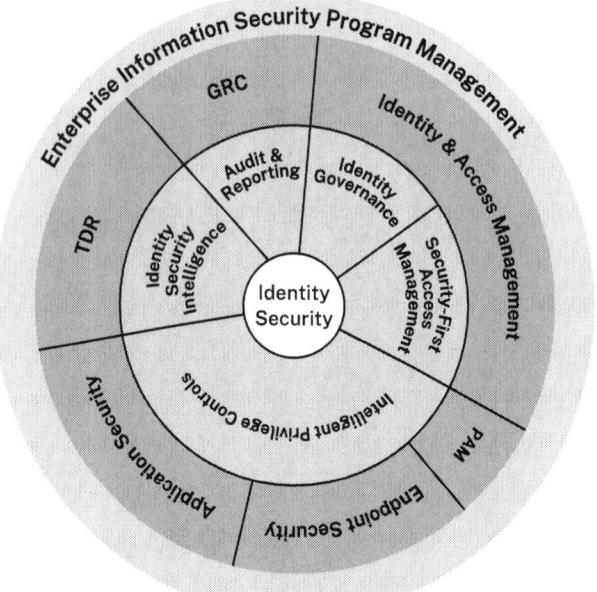

Figure 3-1: Elements of identity security contribute to six cybersecurity domains.

Identity and access management

Within traditional IAM program management, identity security provides identity governance and security-first access management controls. These enable organizations to better control, govern, and certify access to enterprise resources and to ensure that access to enterprise web applications and systems complies with both organizational policies and regulatory compliance mandates.

PAM, endpoint security, and application security

Within PAM, endpoint security, and application security domains, identity security enables organizations to apply the appropriate levels of privilege controls so they can better protect their workforce, IT user, developer, and machine identities. It does this by providing a range of "intelligent privilege controls," which will be discussed in the next chapter.

Some of the ways identity security strengthens PAM, endpoint security, and AppSec include:

- ☑ Ensuring that additional controls are in place to protect high-risk and sensitive enterprise resources
- ☑ Securing endpoints through the removal of local admin rights
- ☑ Protecting browser and credential stores
- ☑ Removing hard-coded secrets from machine workloads

TDR

Identity security tools generate identity-related intelligence that enhances the ability of traditional threat detection and response (TDR) solutions to detect and respond to threats that can:

- ☑ Compromise identities
- ☑ Use these compromised identities to gain a foothold in an organization's infrastructure
- ☑ Move laterally and vertically inside the infrastructure
- ☑ Escalate privileges

GRC

Identity security solutions can bolster governance, risk, and compliance programs by helping them audit and report on identity management and access events. They also provide capabilities to document risk mitigation progress and compliance efforts. These enable internal and external audit teams to respond to GRC and audit requests with speed and efficiency.

ON THE WEB
You can learn more about how identity security strengthens different cybersecurity domains by reading "Understanding the Identity Attack Chain with the CyberArk Blueprint" at https://www.cyberark.com/resources/white-papers/cyberark-blueprint-for-identity-security-success-whitepaper.

Identity Security Program Models

Organizations often operate elements of an identity security program in a silo or with specialization, such as a workstream dedicated to exclusively traditional IAM or secrets management. This siloed approach to execution hampers an organization's ability to strategically mitigate identity risk across all aspects of cybersecurity programs. CISOs should aim to break down these silos and reflect a unified identity security approach as identity crosses the entire organization—it is not just an IT issue. There are two primary ways an identity security program should fit within a cybersecurity program to be most effective.

Freestanding program

The functional restructuring of existing cybersecurity programs can form a new freestanding pillar, whereby the critical functions of the programs above are rolled into one new program. Some areas are more critical to this centralized approach, like traditional IAM, PAM, endpoint and application security. Reactive areas like threat detection and response, the SOC, and GRC are likely to stay independent with stronger relationships to the new program. This approach requires a transformational organizational effort to execute but is the most effective way to manage and implement because of the vertical integration.

The benefit of this approach is a more unified identity security strategy, streamlined operational delivery of identity security controls and a reduction in internal friction and competing priorities amongst peer teams.

Distributed "notional" program

An identity security program can also be structured as a "notional" organization with a matrix management approach. This encourages deeper engagement and relationships across the existing programs to foster more streamlined planning and execution. This structure promotes a "one team, one mission" mindset in which direct reporting structures don't stand in the way of the organization's mission to mitigate identity-related risk. The CISO sets the direction for identity security in collaboration with their extended leadership team, and they use this top-down approach to break down the silo barriers to execute better.

This approach is easier to implement than a freestanding program. However, it requires stronger collaboration, better strategic alignment and planning, and an increased level of accountability to ensure the concept is being executed correctly.

DON'T FORGET

Organizations who are on their journey to implementing zero trust may view this as a "zero trust program"—but you can't do this without identity. Identity security is at the core of an effective zero trust architecture and the program that you build around it. You can't have a zero trust program without an identity security program.

CAUTION

Whether your organization creates a standalone program or a notional one, your teams must adopt and maintain an "identity fabric" mindset to keep up with the paradigm shift that's occurring within the world of identity. Identity plays a key role in so many areas of enterprise information security. Weaving the threads of identity security throughout it is critical to protect against modern identity-based attacks. Otherwise, organizations will continue to function in disjointed silos, failing to mitigate the severity and speed of threats of today.

Eight Qualities of Successful Identity Security Programs

Effective identity security programs embody key characteristics such as executive engagement and integration across security domains without impacting productivity and the user experience.

Successful identity security programs:

1. **Communicate with IT and non-technical managers** to achieve executive buy-in and build support and encouragement from the CISO and line of business executives.

2. **Integrate across information security programs** to facilitate an identity fabric.

3. **Incorporate threat intelligence insights** into the tactics, techniques, and procedures (TTPs) of threat actors to ensure the organization is protected against emerging threats

4. **Leverage leading security frameworks** and regulatory standards to drive a holistic view of cybersecurity, balanced with area-specific frameworks like the CyberArk Blueprint for Identity Security Success (see the *On the Web* paragraph on page 28) to work smarter and faster.

5. **Focus on risk mitigation** first and foremost, with the appropriate level of privilege control for each identity.

6. **Adopt a continuous improvement mindset** and leverage process maturity models (discussed on pages 93 and 94) to build roadmaps toward a comprehensive identity security program.

7. **Establish success metrics** and key performance indicators (KPIs), which leadership will regularly review to maintain alignment with business goals and objectives.

8. **Use automation and orchestration** to accelerate business processes and free humans to solve problems and think strategically using a RACI matrix for smooth execution.

In Chapter 13 we'll examine the elements needed to implement an identity security strategy in your organization.

Takeaways and recommendations

- Identity security is intertwined with IAM, PAM, endpoint security, AppSec, GRC, and other security domains.
- Successful identity security programs require strong executive support and cross-departmental collaboration.
- Top-down encouragement and support are necessary to ensure that all stakeholders understand the importance of identity security and work together to implement it effectively across the organization.
- Organizations must adopt advanced technology solutions such as intelligent privilege controls and continuous threat detection (discussed in the coming chapters) to mitigate identity-related risks.

Chapter 4

Critical Capabilities for an Identity Security Platform

- Understand the key capabilities for an advanced identity security solution
- Learn how CyberArk can help

What criteria should your organization use to select an identity security solution?

Understanding the essential capabilities of a unified identity security platform will empower security practitioners and CISOs to recommend the right solution to achieve business resilience and improve the organization's security posture. In this chapter, we touch on some general selection considerations and key capabilities we think everyone needs.

Characteristics of Advanced Identity Security Solutions

An advanced identity security platform should be holistic and able to manage and secure both human and machine identities across physical, virtual, and cloud environments. The management and security processes for all identity groups need to be unified to help ensure consistent application of policies, drive operational efficiencies, and provide comprehensive visibility into the organization's risk posture.

The platform's capabilities should reduce risks associated with privileged access. It should include MFA, SSO, privileged access management, and identity lifecycle management.

It should also provide advanced services for maintaining tight security controls and compliance standards, such as threat detection, session monitoring, and access reviews.

Advanced solutions should support proactive threat detection by harnessing AI to analyze millions of data points so security practitioners can see problems coming and stop them in their tracks.

Finally, the right platform should be flexible enough to manage and secure diverse environments, from endpoints to cloud platforms and SaaS applications, while catering to the specific needs of any industry, from banking to healthcare and everything in between.

What to Look for in a Platform

Security for workforce, IT user, developer, and machine identities

It's critical to ensure that the right users have secure access to the right resources at the right times. Your platform should make this happen by protecting credentials and tightly controlling access to on-premises and cloud-based applications, services, and IT infrastructure.

Protection of endpoints

Organizations must control unmanaged privileges on endpoints to reduce the attack surface and defend against threats like ransomware. The platform should achieve this by removing local admin rights, enforcing role-specific least privilege, and improving audit readiness.

Scalable privileged access management

Identities and privileges used to maintain, migrate, and scale IT projects are a major source of cybersecurity risk. An identity security platform should support security teams as they discover, secure, and measure these risks. An important consideration for scaling adoption of PAM controls is the ability to apply low-friction privilege controls within an IT user's native tooling for access to Windows, Linux, and database infrastructure, and multi-cloud services.

Integration with existing tools

Tight integration between the platform and a wide range of existing security and IT tools increases visibility into identity-related vulnerabilities, improves detection of attacks, and speeds up containment and remediation. Such integration also provides contextual data for better analysis and planning and protects an organization's existing investment in technology and infrastructure.

A secure browser

By securing browsers—the most heavily used application in the enterprise—with session and cookie theft protection, a platform can provide a higher level of protection than most organizations have today.

Support for new access models

Implementing zero trust access models requires a platform with comprehensive PAM capabilities for operating systems, endpoints, cloud infrastructure, cloud workloads, servers, databases, applications, hypervisors, network devices, and security appliances.

Secrets management

An identity security platform must secure and manage the secrets and credentials used by applications, workloads, and other machine identities to access sensitive resources across both enterprise and external IT environments.

Security for identities in the cloud

Identities for developers, cloud operations personnel, IT users, and machines all have high-risk access privileges. Addressing their different needs and access habits requires a strategy that concentrates resources on the most vulnerable areas. An identity security platform should be designed around a strategy that dovetails with the frameworks of major cloud service providers and complies with relevant regulatory standards.

Automation and orchestration

Management of digital identities should be automated across enterprise IT environments so identity management teams can create, maintain, and analyze access permissions centrally. The identity security platform should leverage automation and orchestration to perform key lifecycle management tasks, especially time-intensive processes such as access provisioning and de-provisioning and detection and response workflows, faster and more accurately than humans can.

How CyberArk Can Help

Centered on intelligent privilege controls, the CyberArk Identity Security Platform seamlessly secures human and machine identities and access to workloads in hybrid and multi-cloud environments. It also flexibly automates the identity lifecycle. All this takes place within a unified solution.

This comprehensive and extensible identity security platform enables zero trust security and enforces least privilege principles across workforce access, endpoint identity security, PAM, secrets management, cloud security, and other identity management domains.

The CyberArk Identity Security Platform uses a modular approach that gives organizations the flexibility to start with best-in-class capabilities such as PAM or implement the entire platform. Organizations that use the CyberArk Identity Security Platform have achieved measurable cyber risk reduction, operational efficiencies, cost savings, and productivity gains.

For more insight into how other organizations used the CyberArk Identity Security Platform to improve their security posture, read Chapter 14. To explore the CyberArk Identity Security Platform, go to: https://www.cyberark.com/products/

 ON THE WEB

IDC has calculated an average annual benefit of $3.1 million from implenting an identity security platform, generating a 309% three-year return on investment. Read the report at: https://www.cyberark.com/resources/white-papers/the-business-value-of-cyberark.

Takeaways and recommendations

- An advanced identity security platform should manage human and machine identities across physical, virtual and cloud environments.

- A comprehensive identity security platform should enable end-to-end security starting with workforce access using a secure browser and encompassing PAM, endpoint security, secrets management, and cloud security.

- An advanced identity security platform should be unified yet modular and able to meet customers where they are, whether starting with one set of solutions such as PAM or implementing the entire suite.

Chapter 5

Overview of Intelligent Privilege Controls

In this chapter

- Define intelligent privilege controls
- See how empathy for end users comes into play
- Explore five essential intelligent privilege controls

What Are Intelligent Privilege Controls?

ntelligent privilege controls are at the center of advanced identity security solutions and best practices. They build on decades of experience with PAM implementations and extend them to meet the needs of today's diverse and dynamic computing environments. They are essential for improving user experiences and meeting the expectations of tech-savvy employees and customers. They are also critical for implementing zero trust concepts.

What are intelligent privilege controls? They are identity security measures that can be applied dynamically to requests to access and interact with enterprise resources. The controls are "intelligent" because their application can be modified in real time, at the start of and during sessions, based on contextual factors such as the requester's level of authorization, the expected user experience, and the risk level of the task at hand.

Empathy for users

One of the defining characteristics of intelligent privilege controls is the ability to take user expectations into account and balance them against risks. Intelligent privilege controls can be applied lightly or not at all when risks are low and ratcheted up appropriately when higher risk levels are assessed. But no matter how that risk fluctuates, the user experience must be consistent.

Five Essential Intelligent Privilege Controls

While there are many intelligent privilege controls (you will see quite a few mentioned in Chapters 7-10), five stand out as being essential for identity security programs:

1. Access with zero standing privileges

2. Vaulting and credential management

3. Session protection, isolation and monitoring

4. Endpoint identity security

5. Identity threat detection and response

Access with Zero Standing Privileges (ZSP)

In the traditional model, privileges and entitlements associated with identities are determined in advance by a manager or some type of role-based access control (RBAC) system and thereafter remain static and "always on." Some users might have more or fewer entitlements than others and be subject to more or fewer controls, but once established, those don't change (unless the manager or RBAC system intervenes).

Zero standing privileges is the security principle that all entitlements should be removed from an identity until temporary access is authorized, usually by some type of risk assessment process. This removal of the traditional persistent "always-on" privileged access approach reflects the paradigm shift in how organizations must secure identities.

In a typical scenario where access with ZSP is applied, a user starts by authenticating to a network or system and requesting temporary alignment with a role or a set of entitlements. The role would have been established previously, constrained by the principle of least privilege, and the request would be time-bound to reduce the exposure to changes in risk over time (say, by a user going on a coffee break and leaving a session running). The user is then granted short-term access based on that role or set of entitlements.

Upon completion of the work, the system enforces the removal of all the entitlements and the user is returned to the default state of zero permissions.

ZSP can also elevate user rights on the fly and then quickly downgrade or revoke them, giving the right level of access to the right person at the right time based on risk at that moment.

ZSP reduces the attack surface in a temporal sense. If an attacker acquires credentials to log into the user's account, the credentials become useless as soon as the session ends, or possibly as soon as contextual factors show that the risk level has increased.

The next access request from that account (from either the real user or the threat actor) will be evaluated based on risk factors, for example, if the request is made from one of the user's typical locations, during their typical work hours, or to access a resource needed for their job. This process also ensures that third-party remote access stays aligned with zero trust and least privilege principles.

ZSP is widely applicable in modern environments because it protects assets in the cloud as well as in a self-hosted infrastructure. In the cloud, organizations can manage on-demand access across the board from one location (utilizing native tools like a browser to gain access to CSP services). Workloads, infrastructure, and instances stay secure, running in AWS, Azure, and Google Cloud Platform (GCP), as VMs and in containers. Organizations that maintain a physical footprint can extend these capabilities to the data center and other self-hosted infrastructure.

ON THE WEB

To learn more about ZSP, read the CyberArk blog post "Zero Standing Privileges: The Essentials" (https://www.cyberark. com/resources/blog/zero-standing-privileges-the-essentials) or watch the video "Implementing Zero Standing Privileges and Just-in-Time-Access" (https://www.cyberark.com/resources/ webinars/implementing-zero-standing-privilege-and- just-in-time-access).

Credential Vaulting and Management

Credential vaulting and management is a set of controls that secure the passwords and keys used by workforce, IT user, developer, and machine identities to access important infrastructure and cloud services, high-risk SaaS applications, and non-enterprise apps.

For human identities, credential vaulting and management, when combined with session controls, enables the delivery of secure standing privilege controls. For non-human identities, when combined with the removal of hard-coded secrets, it enables secrets management controls.

Why is it so essential to safeguard certain credentials? Because business-critical systems, including those in the cloud, come with built-in administrative accounts. Admins need access to these root accounts so they can stand up services when an SSO connection is lost or Active Directory is down. Root accounts give admins (and threat actors who succeed in accessing the root accounts) immense power, including the power to reconfigure or shut down critical services.

Credential vaulting is the process of storing strings used for authentication within a secure repository. The repository encrypts the credentials, provides non-repudiation (that is, prevents them from being altered surreptitiously by an unknown party), and enforces access control. Credential vaulting serves as a backbone for all other aspects of security: without storing credentials in a secure repository, organizations cannot enforce other controls. It also underlies other controls that reduce the risk of identity compromise, such as credential rotation and isolation.

Credential rotation shortens passwords' time-to-live by automatically changing password values based on a defined security policy or by triggering a manual change process. With rotation, threat actors who acquire credentials such as passwords left behind in hashes or logs find that they become useless after a short period.

Other credential management controls include:

- ☑ **Credential store protection,** which prevents malware from stealing secrets from credential stores such as the Windows LSASS process and the Google Chrome Password Store.

- ☑ **Credential isolation,** which ensures that credentials are separated from a user's workstation (and from users themselves), employs bastion hosts that establish sessions to the target resource without requiring the user to know the password.

- ☑ **Hard-coded credential removal,** which deletes credentials from .ini files, removes user and pass values and environment variables left in code, and erases other sensitive information that developers inadvertently leave behind.

- ☑ **Randomized local credentials,** which obstruct lateral and vertical movement by applying randomized values to local endpoints and systems, ensuring that local account passwords cannot be reused from system to system.

Session Protection, Isolation, and Monitoring

Session protection, isolation, and monitoring controls ensure the integrity of privileged and high-risk sessions connecting with enterprise resources, including resources in cloud platforms, elastic and static infrastructure, and high-risk SaaS applications. They prevent external malicious actors from compromising identities and moving laterally and deter insiders from abusing privileges.

Controls in this category include:

☑ **Session protection,** which guards the client side of web browser-based sessions by blocking file downloads from the web app, access to the clipboard, and drag-and-drop and right-click access to the context menu. It can also protect the Chrome process from being manipulated or abused by unauthorized applications.

☑ **Session isolation,** which ensures that RDP, SSH, web and other sessions connecting users to target resources are isolated from the users' workstations. It also ensures that users access only the specific resources they need and can't move laterally to perform malicious actions against other resources.

☑ **Session monitoring,** which ensures that audit logs and session activity are automatically analyzed to determine whether an identity is performing unauthorized or suspicious actions such as session escapes, unauthorized new user creations, and attempts to move laterally or vertically throughout the environment.

Together, these mechanisms defend against multiple types of pre- and post-authentication attacks and prevent the spread of malware—without sacrificing user experiences.

Endpoint Identity Security

Endpoints, including computers, workstations, mobile devices, and servers, are devices or systems that serve as entry points into a network.

Endpoint identity security controls greatly reduce the risk of ransomware and help reinforce other intelligent privilege controls by enforcing the principle of least privilege and enabling application controls and credential protection on endpoints.

Endpoint identity security controls include:

☑ **Enforcement of least privilege** on endpoints, which ensures that users only receive permissions to access the resources they need to perform their jobs; least privilege policies can be tailored to each user's role.

☑ **Application controls,** which mitigate attacks at the endpoint by intelligently identifying and blocking malicious applications and software and forcing unknown applications to run in a restricted mode with no access to the enterprise network ("graylisting" or "sandboxing").

☑ **Credential protection,** which uses targeted behavioral analytics to detect credential theft attempts at the endpoint level, then automatically removes users from the local administrator group, isolates unknown applications, and manages privilege escalations based on policy. These measures prevent unauthorized access to passwords, credentials, hashes, cookies, and other security tokens stored in the operating system and third-party credential stores.

Identity Threat Detection and Response (ITDR)

Identity threat detection and response uses behavioral analysis to find identity-related threats in sessions and computing environments and responds with automated actions such as continuous and step-up MFA and session termination.

A key ITDR capability is scanning logs from various endpoints and sources before and after login processes to detect signs of compromise, suspicious behavior, and malicious actions such as abuses of privileges and attempts to circumvent security controls.

For example, when users' activities are flagged as risky, they might temporarily lose privileged access to enterprise resources until an investigation is complete. This intervention helps prevent identity compromise, stop lateral and vertical movement, and cut off privilege abuse.

Controls in this category include:

☑ **Continuous authentication,** which prompts users to re-authenticate their sessions through a defined set of authentication factors based on ongoing risk assessments throughout the session. It can prevent privilege abuse by ensuring that idle user sessions cannot be compromised by malicious actors lurking on machines and attempting to impersonate the user.

☑ **Step-up authentication,** where users are asked to supply additional steps for authentication based on the nature of their requests and detection of risk factors such as deviation from the user's customary location, IP address, or workstation.

☑ **Session termination,** which automatically responds to instances of suspicious or malicious behavior by terminating sessions in progress or automatically onboarding privileged credentials that were created out-of-band.

Intelligent privilege controls within an integrated identity security framework are not just about tightening security. In a fast-paced world, they can strengthen oversight, control, and analytics without slowing down users. By adopting these advanced controls and practices, organizations can protect their most sensitive digital assets while ensuring operational efficiency and regulatory compliance.

TIP ITDR should extend beyond mere monitoring of the vendor infrastructure or Active Directory. It should offer a comprehensive view of all identities within an organization. Also, integrating ITDR within a unified identity security platform is a more coherent and holistic approach than tacking on an additional solution. That integration allows for a consistent record of identity, which is crucial to ensure that security measures remain effective across different platforms and services.

Examples of step-up authentication

Let's say that a user identity pops up during non-work hours, from an unusual account, using the wrong password. A step-up authentication process might use AI to organize the information, measure the level of risk, correlate additional controls with the risk, and prompt the user for more authentication. The MFA process issues security prompts only when necessary and delivers optimized security without annoying users.

Now let's say a user wants to request additional permission to perform an important business task. Rather than making the user email an admin, who then must analyze the user's usage patterns and contact her manager for approval, a step-up authentication tool with AI might perform the analysis, assess the risk, and immediately grant the requested permissions (assuming the risk level was below a pre-determined threshold). This approach makes the user happier and more productive, saves the time of the admin and the user's manager, and automatically creates a full audit trail.

Takeaways and recommendations

- Intelligent privilege controls dynamically adjust access based on real-time risk assessments. These controls help ensure that identities have the right level of access without hindering productivity.
- Key controls include access with zero standing privileges, vaulting and credential management, session protection, isolation and monitoring, endpoint identity security, and identity threat detection and response.

II. Securing the Full Spectrum
of Identities

Chapter 6

Understanding
Identity-related Risk

In this chapter

- Examine the three factors that most influence identity-related risk
- Learn how the risk profiles of the four identity groups can help organizations design tailored identity security policies

What You Need to Know About Identity-related Risk

A foundational concept in the new paradigm of identity security is the idea of applying appropriate security controls based on risks associated with each identity. Certain identities tend to be higher risk or lower risk depending on several factors. Understanding the level of risk for an identity enables us to manage identity security based on the concept of minimum effective control: put appropriate controls in place in accordance with risk, but don't overburden users or operations and administrative teams.

Figure 6-1 illustrates this concept: identity groups whose activities involve less risk typically require fewer controls.

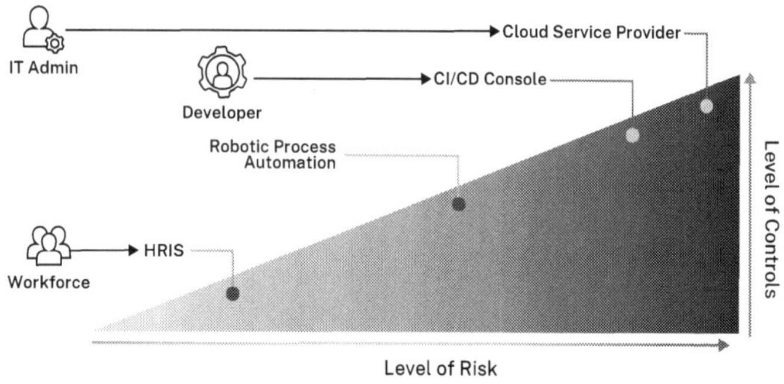

Figure 6-1: The concept of minimum effective control.

Because identity-related risk is so central to identity security, it is important to understand:

1. The factors that influence identity-related risk

2. The risk profiles of our four identity groups (workforce, IT user, developer, and machine)

Factors That Influence Identity-related Risk

Risk can be defined in many ways depending on the context, situation and organization. Many factors influence risk and the methods to calculate it, such as data classification, data sensitivity, and monetary impact.

In the context of identity security, we can define risk as the sum of three factors that are common to all organizations and widely exploited by malicious actors. As shown in Figure 6-2, these are:

1. Level of privilege

2. Scope of influence

3. Ease of compromise

The larger each of these values is, the larger its impact. The larger the impact, the larger the risk. The larger the risk, the more risk mitigation that is required.

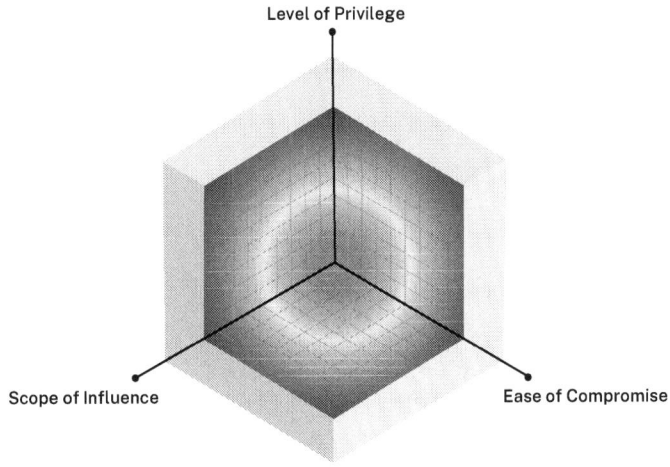

Figure 6-2: The three primary factors of identity-related risk.

Level of privilege

Level of privilege refers to the type of privileged actions identities can perform against given resources. Specific privileges and entitlements vary from system to system, but generally consist of a spectrum that includes:

- ☑ Read-only
- ☑ Read-write
- ☑ Service-level administrator
- ☑ Modify user permissions
- ☑ Full administrator permissions

Read-only access is the least risky permission since identities with that permission can't modify or add data. In contrast, modify user permissions might allow identities to escalate their own (and others') privileges. Full administrator permissions create the highest level of risk. The higher the level of privilege granted to an identity, the higher the level of risk it poses, because it has a greater ability to change data and grant itself additional powers.

Scope of influence

Scope of influence, also referred to as the blast radius, refers to the number or percentage of systems an identity or account can access, either directly or indirectly; perhaps one or 10 resources, or 10% or 100% of all resources of a certain type. The larger the scope of influence, the higher the level of risk the identity poses.

When thinking about the scope of influence, it's important to remember how interconnected and hierarchical IT and enterprise resources can be. You'll often need to think about access in terms of a specific resource type (e.g., Windows servers), or more broadly, multiple types of resources, or even all resources (e.g., access to all elastic workloads in the cloud or all cloud-native services).

Another consideration is "downstream" or "inherited" access. When identities are granted privileges for a given resource, will that resource provide subsequent access to other systems?

CAUTION

Always be alert for identities with a high scope of influence. They can impact a wide swath of other systems and need to be protected and managed accordingly. For example, an identity with administrative access to an automation service like Terraform will have downstream administrative permissions to important IT systems for infrastructure-as-code automation.

Ease of compromise

Ease of compromise refers to how easy or challenging it is for a malicious actor to compromise an identity. It can be assessed by examining factors like:

- ☑ Common patterns or attacks on that identity
- ☑ Technical vulnerabilities related to the identity
- ☑ Access or resources that threat actors can exploit
- ☑ Poor internal processes that expose the identity
- ☑ The type and quality of controls protecting the identity

Test Your Knowledge: Rate the Risk Factors!

Round 1: Domain Admin Login to Workstations

A Domain Administrator account has administrative privileges to all the servers and workstations in the environment. The workstations of workforce users tend to be the main landing place for malicious actors. Because of how Windows authentication works, a Domain Administrator privileged account that logged into workstations will leave credential residues in the form of hashes that could be exploited by a bad actor. Rate the risk factors!

	Low	Medium	High
Level of privilege	[ ]	[ ]	[ ]
Scope of influence	[ ]	[ ]	[ ]
Ease of compromise	[ ]	[ ]	[ ]

Round 2: SMS-based MFA for IdP Access to Cloud Services

An organization leverages SMS-based MFA for identity provider federated access into cloud service providers. SMS-based MFA is considered weak and easily bypassed via TTPs like SIM swap fraud, phishing attacks and SS7 interception. Using freestanding permissions for these identities means that the permissions can be immediately exploited by bad actors. Administrator-type users of the cloud service providers would be particularly vulnerable to attacks. Rate the risk factors!

	Low	Medium	High
Level of privilege	[ ]	[ ]	[ ]
Scope of influence	[ ]	[ ]	[ ]
Ease of compromise	[ ]	[ ]	[ ]

Round 3: Manual Onboarding Processes for Privileged Accounts

An organization that uses a standard server build image sets the built-in administrator accounts, a Windows Administrator (SID-500) and a UNIX Root (UID0), to a default password (although they rename the default username). They have a manual process to identify newly created servers. This requires their privileged accounts to be protected post-creation, which results in a delay in time-to-protection and gives malicious actors an extended window to potentially compromise those accounts. Rate the risk factors!

	Low	Medium	High
Level of privilege	[ ]	[ ]	[ ]
Scope of influence	[ ]	[ ]	[ ]
Ease of compromise	[ ]	[ ]	[ ]

The answers (don't peek)
Round 1: High, High, Medium / **Round 2:** High, High, High / **Round 3:** High, High, Medium

Identity Groups Have Distinct Risk Profiles

In theory, you might want to tailor a customized set of identity security controls for every identity in your enterprise. In practice, you need to start with a small number of templates that apply to large groups of identities and customize those for smaller groups and individual identities as time and resources permit.

Fortunately (and not coincidentally), the four identity groups we described earlier—workforce, IT user, developer, and machine—provide just such templates. Each one has a distinct set of characteristics, identity security requirements, and appropriate intelligent privilege controls that can be used to design tailored identity security policies and workflows.

We will be exploring exactly those details in the next four chapters.

Obviously, there is a great deal of variation within those identity groups, but experience has shown that using them as starting points dramatically simplifies the process of aligning controls with risks.

Takeaways and recommendations

- Identity-related risk is determined by three main factors: the level of privilege, the scope of influence (or the number of systems an identity can access), and the ease of compromise. The greater these factors, the higher the risk.

- Our four identity groups have distinct risk profiles. Using them as templates can dramatically simplify the process of aligning controls and risks for large numbers of identities across an enterprise.

Chapter 7

Workforce Identities

In this chapter

- See who is included in the workforce
- Learn the identity security requirements and appropriate intelligent privilege controls for workforce identities

Who Are Workforce Users?

Workforce users are employees, temporary contractors, partners, application administrators and any other users who need access to an organization's internal resources. They engage with a variety of endpoints, data, and applications to perform their daily tasks. The primary entry point for most of their interactions is a web browser with the method for accessing all resources taking place at the endpoint.

The risk level of workforce users fluctuates with their access privileges and the scope of their duties. For instance, finance and HR employees manage essential data, while application admins possess elevated privileges that give them control over (and the power to disrupt) critical business processes. This puts them under the traditional definition of privileged users who have long been top targets of malicious actors. And, as we mentioned in an earlier chapter, the boundaries between privileged users and others have blurred, with many "ordinary" users occasionally accessing sensitive data and systems and engaging in other high-risk activities.

Identity Security Requirements for Workforce Users

Most cyberattacks start on endpoints. Every human identity in the enterprise connects to resources using a workstation with built-in local admin accounts and complex entitlements, whether that device is owned by the enterprise or the employee.

Yet far too often, employee devices are not protected from common identity-based attacks that exploit built-in privileged access. Neglecting these issues can lead to a weakened security stance, expanded attack surfaces, and the perpetual threat of non-compliance. Therefore, organizations need to ensure that the complete user session is secure. This includes the first mile of access via managed and unmanaged endpoints to on-premises resources, cloud platforms, and SaaS applications, to the last mile of data consumption via the browser.

At the same time, employees need to be able to securely connect to enterprise applications and resources from all their devices at all hours without hitting tons of roadblocks. Organizations must navigate a balance between security and productivity to avoid a backlash from frustrated employees who feel they can't perform their duties.

A proactive, identity-centric approach to workforce identity security must protect both enterprise-managed and unmanaged endpoints and servers from common attack vectors and critical ransomware entry points, such as drive-by malware downloads, malicious email attachments, and credential compromise. To limit the attack surface and prevent zero-day attacks, identity-security tools need to apply least privilege principles for users and machines.

Key Intelligent Privilege Controls for Workforce Users

Workforce users and their data and devices need to be protected by intelligent privilege controls that:

- ☑ Provide an end-to-end passwordless experience from the endpoint and browser to every application and resource.

- ☑ Record, monitor, and analyze user actions pre- and post- login and enforce identity security policies continuously, at scale, with input from artificial intelligence.

- ☑ Leverage real-time user behavior analytics and identity threat detection and response.

- ☑ Use a native no-code automation engine to accelerate processes for managing identity security controls across the complete user lifecycle, from onboarding and provisioning, through job and role changes, to de-provisioning and removal.

- ☑ Manage workforce passwords securely during the transition to passwordless environments and integrate with credential management and SSO tools to enhance security and user experiences.

- ☑ Provide visibility and control over web application sessions, enabling monitoring and compliance of passwordless sessions through session recording and user behavior analysis.

- ☑ Automate the management of the user lifecycle across systems, ensuring that only authorized users have access, and their permissions are updated in real-time to maintain security and compliance.

- ☑ Securely manage privileged access, enforce least privilege on servers and endpoints, support passwordless access and reduce the risk of credential misuse.

Takeaways and recommendations

- Most workforce users present low or medium risk, but many sometimes require high levels of privilege, which blurs the line between privileged and "ordinary" users.

- Organizations must ensure that security measures do not hinder employee productivity.

- A proactive, identity-centric approach should include least privilege and intelligent privilege controls that protect against attacks while maintaining a low-friction user experience.

Chapter 8

IT User Identities

In this chapter

- See who is an IT user in the context of identity security
- Learn the identity security requirements and appropriate intelligent privilege controls for IT user identities

Who Are IT Users?

For the purposes of identity security, IT users consist of traditional IT administrators, third-party vendors and contractors, and admins for cloud operations, applications, and security operations. This identity group has evolved beyond traditional roles like Windows, Linux, and database admins, and now includes the administrators working with cloud services, managing DevOps tools, and operating cybersecurity services.

IT users have access to a wide variety of privileged environments. These include:

☑ High-risk SaaS applications

☑ Cybersecurity tools such as identity security, ITDR, and vulnerability management services

☑ Automation and continuous delivery/continuous deployment (CI/CD) tools like Terraform and Ansible

☑ Cloud-native services like serverless compute functions and container services

☑ Elastic cloud workloads such as virtual machines and databases

☑ IT users control parameters and configurations of long-lived systems, including those for

☑ Domain Admin and Server Admin access

☑ Access to Windows, Unix and Linux servers, databases, and other networking and infrastructure devices.

The access pattern for IT users means that they have very high levels of privilege and a wide scope of influence across the entire enterprise, making it critical to protect their identities, workstations, and enterprise resources.

Identity Security Requirements for IT Users

Today's IT users are responsible for enterprise resources that range from legacy mainframes to cloud service providers.

To build, migrate, scale and operate IT systems, your IT users, both permanent staff members and third-party contractors, need administrative access. For maximum efficiency, this access must be secured with as little disruption to the user experience as possible. Among the key requirements:

☑ Workflows that enable fast, frictionless access to the tools IT users need

☑ Integration of those workflows with existing admin tools

☑ Native access using preferred connection clients like RDP, PuTTY, and Cloud CLIs

Key Intelligent Privilege Controls for IT Users

The work of IT users should be protected by intelligent privilege controls that include:

- ☑ Central discovery, vaulting, and management of all admin credentials to defend against credential theft
- ☑ Federated zero standing privileges access for admins managing cloud workloads and services
- ☑ Session isolation, monitoring, auditing, and analytics within native UX (RDP, SSH, SQL, Cloud CLIs, SaaS & IaaS consoles), to reduce the risk of compromised access and malware spread
- ☑ Built-in low and no-code automation engines, to simplify provisioning and de-provisioning admin tasks

Takeaways and recommendations

- IT users now encompass internal and external staff with a broad range of responsibilities and access to a variety of privileged environments, making them a critical identity group.
- To secure IT users, organizations need intelligent privilege controls such as centralized credential management and session isolation, as well as automation of identity security workflows and integration with existing admin tools.

Chapter 9

Developer Identities

- See who counts as a developer for the purposes of identity security
- Learn the identity security requirements and appropriate intelligent privilege controls for developer identities

Who Are Developers?

Developers include a broad spectrum of "builder" and "coder" positions, including:

- ☑ Software engineers
- ☑ Software and application architects
- ☑ Application testers
- ☑ DevSecOps team members
- ☑ Site reliability engineers
- ☑ Data scientists

Developer workstations host a variety of passwords, credentials, workload source code, and privileges that enable developers to access their downstream enterprise resources. These include artifacts like the browser password store, session cookies, local security authority subsystem service (LSASS) processes, remote desktop connection management (RDCM) tools, software development tools, and local admin rights.

DevOps admins and developers need access to many of the same infrastructure and cloud services management tools as IT users. But there's an important difference: *developers control the source code of the workloads* that they develop. They can alter these workloads and the associated data, applications, and code. Their right to modify code and their always-on access to the cloud introduce significant risks and complexities in balancing security against user productivity and the need to fix software defects quickly.

In addition, developers are responsible for protecting machine identity workloads. They must be able to configure security controls that implement application security checks and procedures and handle secrets management for machine identities.

DevOps admins and developers can also access a wide variety of privileged environments, including high-risk SaaS applications, cloud services, and long-lived systems. High-risk SaaS applications include automation and CI/CD tools like Jenkins, Terraform and Ansible, and development tools like Data Dog and Postman.

Securing developer identities and their workloads is critical for protecting against software supply chain attacks like the SolarWinds attack in 2020, which introduced malicious software into thousands of organizations. This type of threat is only going to increase. According to "The World Will Store 200 Zettabytes of Data by 2025" report from Cybersecurity Ventures, 338 billion lines of new software code will need to be secured by 2025.

Identity Security Requirements for Developers

Velocity is an important metric in software development. For rapid delivery of software features and functions, developers need low-friction authentication and quick approval of their requests for additional access. Organizations that slow down these processes risk disrupting innovation, delaying fixes to application outages, and hampering the growth of the entire enterprise.

In the public cloud environments where most developers work, access to systems is federated via IAM roles, not provisioned through shared accounts and passwords. Cloud providers recommend that organizations minimize the use of shared credentials wherever possible, instead using federated access to IAM roles for security purposes and to expedite access to shifting targets that spin up and down depending on demand and application traffic.

The need for developers to obtain admin-type access creates a need to secure privileged access in federated workflows. The cloud has driven a major evolution in the provisioning of privileged access.

Developers need privileged access to admin roles to manage:

- ☑ Cloud-native services governing customer-facing applications
- ☑ Cloud workloads like elastic VMs, databases, and Kubernetes containers
- ☑ Web applications such as PagerDuty, Datadog, and Confluence

Secure access for hybrid and multi-cloud environments based on the principles of least privilege and zero standing privileges allows data scientists and cloud engineers to work natively and efficiently. Seamless integration with DevOps workflows enables dynamic, just-in-time access that doesn't slow productivity.

Meanwhile, as developers code, they create machine identities and application secrets—all of which must also be secured to protect against credential theft. In fact, secrets management should sync with native tools for secure retrieval without changing workflows.

Figure 9-1 shows the range of tools and applications used in developing and deploying web applications, and how identity security controls help control both human and machine access at each step of the development lifecycle.

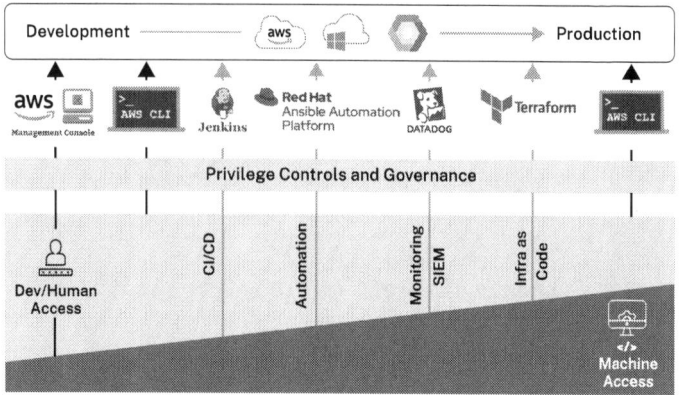

Figure 9-1: Identity security controls are needed at each step of the development lifecycle.

Key Intelligent Privilege Controls for Developers

Developer security and productivity depends on intelligent privilege controls that provide:

- ☑ Zero standing privileges (ZSP) access to admin roles for cloud-native services and workloads

- ☑ Time, entitlements, and approvals (TEA) concepts that reduce the risk of access to all systems and environments

- ☑ Seamless user experiences with Cloud CLIs, web consoles, SSH, RDP, SQL, kubectl, and session auditing tools

- ☑ ChatOps-based access requests and automated approval workflows to accelerate provisioning of emergency access

Securing cloud identities

Protecting the cloud is a shared responsibility, and protecting the identities in the cloud falls upon you. It must be performed holistically.

Securing access to cloud-native services and workloads also requires an organization to understand the various methods of authentication and authorization to help protect the compromise of your cloud identities from bad actors. Want to learn more about securing cloud identities? Follow the corresponding URL to discover additional content: Best Practices for Securing Cloud Identities: A CyberArk Blueprint Whitepaper (https://www. cyberark.com/resources/white-papers/best-practices-for-securing-cloud-identities-a-cyberark-blueprint-whitepaper).

Takeaways and recommendations

- DevOps admins and developers hold high levels of privilege and control over critical resources to manage CI/CD pipelines and build processes. They require always-on access to the cloud environments in which they work. They are a high-risk identity group that must be secured to ensure that the deployed software is secure and to prevent software supply chain attacks.
- Developers and cloud operations teams require seamless and efficient access to ensure productivity and velocity.
- Implementing secure access controls like ZSP is essential for maintaining security without disrupting innovation or delaying critical fixes.

Chapter 10

Machine Identities

In this chapter

- Understand which software and hardware "machines" have identities that must be managed
- Learn the identity security requirements and appropriate intelligent privilege controls for machine identities

What Are Machine Identities?

In the context of identity security, "machine identities" are the identities of software workloads, applications, devices, and other non-human entities like AI agents. Sometimes they are referred to as "non-human identities" or NHIs.

Today, machine identities far outnumber human identities and, according to the CyberArk 2024 Identity Security Threat Report, their proliferation makes them the No. 1 driver of identity growth.

Software and hardware "machines"

Machine identities include IT infrastructure as well as software and cloud workloads (including cloud provider services and third-party commercial, internally developed, and open-source software), bots, AI agents, and other software objects and devices. Whether built, bought, or borrowed, these workloads provide a wide variety of functions. They include:

☑ Security tools

☑ Business applications

☑ Automation and CI/CD tools

☑ Cloud-native services

☑ Dynamic and ephemeral workloads

☑ Static, OS-based workloads

Of course, industrial manufacturing equipment (such as gas turbines for electricity generation, milling machines, etc.) can also have machine identities. These include computers, sensors, and controllers that are part of operational technology (OT) and industrial control systems (ICS), as well as the exploding quantity of Internet of Things (IoT) devices.

Special machine identity challenges

These diverse types of machines have something in common—almost all of them access or are accessed by enterprise resources, including devices, data, apps, and infrastructure.

The access patterns for machines mean that they often have very high levels of privilege, a very wide scope of influence, and access to mission-critical and sensitive data across the entire enterprise. They also require secrets and credentials to authenticate and authorize their access. As the number of machine identities grows, so does the challenge of managing their secrets and credentials.

While there is overlap between the processes for managing human and machine identities, they are more challenging for machine identities and often require different capabilities. Attackers don't care if an identity is human or machine; they will exploit and move between human and machine identities to access and steal the organization's data and resources. For example, in cloud environments, new workloads and compute instances are dynamically created to meet the needs of the business and then terminated when no longer needed. But when machine identities are created on demand for these workloads and instances, where do they get their authentication secrets and access credentials?

In a Kubernetes environment, for example, when a new container instance is created, it will likely need certificates and secrets to be dynamically created to authenticate the new container's identity to other containers, and to provide the secrets to access other workloads and resources.

Unfortunately, even today these secrets and credentials may be embedded, or hard coded, into the source code, even though the risks of this practice are now widely understood. For example, once a secret is hard coded, it may be considered too operationally risky to rotate it because of the possibility that changing the credential would break an unknown production system that uses it.

Additionally, source code is often stored in code repositories (so that it can be shared across developers), but if it is hard coded and if the repository gives public access, then the secrets and other credentials, such as cloud access keys, are exposed and likely to be stolen.

Instead, organizations should use solutions that centrally manage, rotate, and secure the secrets required by machine identities, providing the workload with the secret needed to access the resource through an API or native capability. Similarly, certificate lifecycle management solutions can assign certificates when needed and ensure certificates are kept up-to-date and secured to prevent operational outages and ensure secure authentication.

Identity Security Requirements for Machine Identities

Organizations need to enforce standardized security policies and interfaces across the enterprise to help prevent outages, downtime, and business disruptions. This mandate should include centralized management of secrets with both rotation and the use of dynamic secrets for all application and workload types, including third-party software, as well as certificate lifecycle management and PKI modernization.

Security teams need to discover secrets in cloud service providers' built-in (native) secrets stores, such as AWS Secrets Manager or Azure Key Vault, to ensure they know what they are responsible for managing.

To simplify developer adoption, secrets management capabilities need to be integrated into existing developer workflows to provide flexible access to secrets for applications and workloads. This might include API access to secrets, native access to out-of-the-box integrations with widely used container platforms and environments (e.g., Kubernetes Secrets, Red Hat OpenShift), and robust tools with APIs to enable automation across all processes.

In many organizations, security teams must do more with less. Inadequate systems and manual processes often prevent potential efficiency gains. This means it is necessary to automate certificate lifecycle management from the initial request to installation and to streamline operations with self-service capabilities, as well as to leverage an integrated ecosystem to reduce human errors and prevent outages and disruptions.

Outdated PKI solutions place an unnecessary burden on security teams, as they are unable to meet the security and renewal requirements of modern applications and cloud environments. Additionally, outdated systems have limited automation capabilities, and their operation often requires a specialist with hard-to-find expertise.

Manual certificate management approaches lead to unnecessary human errors, additional risks, and burdensome security costs that could be avoided with automated systems. Automated mechanisms for certificate management are desirable because of the increasing complexity of multi-cloud environments, the surge in machine identities, and the accelerated pace of certificate renewals.

Automated certificate management approaches can provide significant cost savings, free up vast amounts of time for other IT projects, and offer compelling ROIs. Organizations should adopt a modern PKI solution to replace legacy ones to scale and meet the demands of complex, multi-cloud environments and mobile devices. Other benefits include reducing enterprise PKI costs and complexity.

Key Intelligent Privilege Controls for Machine Identities

Interactions with machine identities should be protected by intelligent privilege controls that include:

- ☑ Policy-based management and rotation of secrets and certificates across all application and workload types
- ☑ Just-in-time or dynamic secrets to provide ephemeral access
- ☑ Strong authentication and authorization for applications, workloads, containers, etc.
- ☑ Support for role-based access controls, zero trust, auditing, and analytics
- ☑ Ability to seamlessly apply privilege controls to machine identities that require access to privileged credentials to perform their functions.

Takeaways and recommendations

- Machine identities, which include workloads, applications, and devices, are rapidly increasing in number. Attackers exploit gaps in machine identities to access high-value resources.

- Machine identities often have high levels of privilege and access to mission-critical resources across the enterprise, making them one of the riskiest identity groups.

- Automating certificate management results in fewer errors, stays current with shrinking certificate validity periods, and avoids squandering precious security team resources that can be deployed to other tasks.

- Different approaches, such as centralized secrets management, dynamic secrets rotation, and strong authentication mechanisms, are required to secure machine identities.

III. Implementing an Identity Security Program

Chapter 11

How Identity Security Enables Zero Trust

■ Explore the connection between identity security and zero trust

ffective identity security is a prerequisite for successful zero trust initiatives. Here we explore how identity security supports zero trust principles and processes.

Least privilege access

The principle of least privilege is one of the fundamental tenets of zero trust architectures. Organizations that apply this principle dramatically reduce the number of entitlements that threat actors can use to access resources and move laterally across environments. Identity security enables security teams to apply least privilege by:

☑ Deepening the analysis of entity roles and data access requirements

☑ Improving real-time evaluations of contextual risk and behavior so security policy controls can be strictly enforced

Use of behavioral data and context

In zero trust models, understanding the context of access requests is as essential as verifying credentials. Contextual and behavioral data provides insights into whether an access request is legitimate or potentially malicious. This data includes user behavior patterns, access time, network location, and the type and security posture of the device making the request. Identity security helps organizations collect and analyze this information so they can make better decisions about allowing or denying access.

Continuous verification

Continuous verification is another core zero trust principle. It requires implementing robust authentication mechanisms and continually revalidating the security posture of each request to access a resource, both at the beginning of each session and throughout its duration. Identity security solutions contribute to ongoing security posture assessments by capturing and analyzing activities associated with identity-related attacks.

Micro-segmentation

Micro-segmentation is a technique used to divide networks into smaller, more-manageable sections with well-defined access limits to minimize lateral movement by an attacker. Identity security helps security teams identify and remove excess permissions, so when an identity is compromised, its "blast radius" (the scope of permitted lateral movement) is greatly reduced. In addition, identity security capabilities such as continuous authentication and adaptive access controls ensure that access to network segments and movement within them are granted based on real-time evaluations of trust.

 ON THE WEB

Want to learn more about zero trust? Follow the corresponding URL to discover additional content: "Guiding Your Leadership Team Through the Zero Trust Mindset" (https://www.cyberark.com/resources/white-papers/guiding-your-leadership-team-through-the-zero-trust-mindset).

Chapter 12

Cybersecurity Frameworks, Regulations, and Insurance

In this chapter

- Review the pros and cons of cybersecurity frameworks, regulations, and insurance requirements
- Note their common controls and requirements
- Understand why you should consider frameworks and standards floors, not ceilings

U p to now, you've gained a good understanding of identity security and its role in improving an organization's security risk posture. In this chapter, we examine the requirements for identity security controls in cybersecurity frameworks, regulatory standards, and cyber insurance underwriting. We also discuss what they don't address in this new paradigm shift, and why you need to go beyond them to create a comprehensive identity security program.

Cybersecurity Frameworks

Cybersecurity frameworks (CSFs) such as NIST CSF 2.0, ISO/ISC 27001, CSA CMM, and COBIT, are extremely helpful in guiding the direction of cybersecurity programs and highlighting key controls that should be put in place. They suggest technical and procedural controls across a wide range of cybersecurity domains (see Figure 12-1).

NIST 800-171	NIST CSF 2.0	NIST 800-207
CIS CSC V8	CSA CMM	HITRUST
ISO/ISC 27001	SOGP	SCF
COBIT	COSO	NSCS CAF

Figure 12-1: Recommended cybersecurity frameworks.

In the case of identity security, CSFs typically include recommended controls related to:

- ☑ Access management
- ☑ Multifactor authentication (MFA)
- ☑ Privilege controls
- ☑ Auditing and accountability

Shortcomings of CSFs

However, CSFs provide little or no guidance on many important topics. For example, they typically don't tell us how to:

- ☑ Manage the implementation of controls and best practices
- ☑ Apply appropriate privilege controls to the different groups of identities and resources in our organizations
- ☑ Improve our identity security processes and mature our cybersecurity program over time.

ON THE WEB Many of the topics mentioned above are addressed in area-specific frameworks like the "CyberArk Blueprint for Identity Security Success" (https://www.cyberark.com/resources/white-papers/cyberark-blueprint-for-identity-security-success-whitepaper).

Regulatory Standards

Regulatory standards and CSFs are sometimes lumped together, but there is a major difference.

CSFs consist of recommendations and guidelines and, except for special circumstances, their provisions are not binding. In contrast, regulatory standards, although often derived from CSFs, are mandatory. Organizations are subject to monetary fines and other penalties for non-compliance.

However, regulatory standards are similar to CSFs in that they are vague in many areas and silent on some important topics. These regulatory standards are required by the government to satisfy audit and compliance requirements as shown in Figure 12-2.

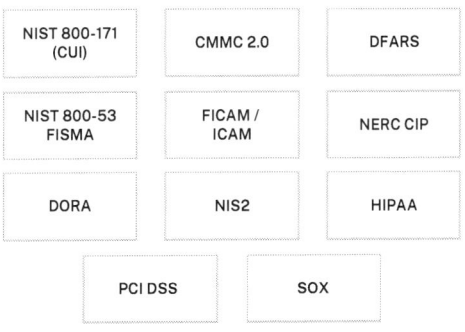

Figure 12-2: Regulatory standards.

Cyber Insurance Underwriting

Cyber insurance coverage has become a must-have for many organizations. Practically speaking, security teams have no choice but to comply with whatever requirements insurance underwriters place on them as conditions of issuing a policy.

The process of working with an underwriter and documenting the organization's compliance with insurance company requirements is akin to working with an auditor or regulator.

Common cyber insurance requirements include:

- ☑ Use of MFA, especially for accounts and cloud IAM roles with highly privileged access
- ☑ Secure management of sensitive passwords and credentials
- ☑ Proactive and reactive controls on laptops and workstations to protect against ransomware attacks
- ☑ Security awareness and training programs
- ☑ Documented incident response plans
- ☑ Backup and recovery plans

Common Controls and Requirements

Despite subtle variations in identity security requirements across various CSFs, regulatory standards, and cyber insurance guidelines, there are many common elements.

Access and lifecycle management

Organizations are required to manage access centrally, ensure that only authorized identities can access systems and data (that is, they must enforce the principle of least privilege access), and establish processes to grant and revoke access when workers are hired, change roles, and are terminated.

Multi-factor authentication

More than one method of authentication must be used to verify the identity of users requesting access to sensitive information on both remote and local networks and systems.

Intelligent privilege controls

Security teams should implement controls that limit user access rights to the minimum necessary. Other requirements include managing and protecting administrative privileges, workstations, and infrastructure, monitoring and controlling privileged sessions, and enforcing separation of duties.

Accountability, auditing, and ITDR

Organizations must collect and retain audit logs for reporting identity and system activity, correlate audit reviews and analysis for reporting purposes, and monitor for anomalous behavior.

Advanced identity security solutions provide security controls and processes for all these identity-related requirements. They address all identities and all types of resources, provide proactive and reactive controls, and secure identity-related lifecycles and processes.

The Paradigm Shift Goes Beyond the Frameworks

Although organizations must pay close attention to CSFs, regulatory standards, and insurance requirements, they should never rely exclusively on them for guidance toward the new paradigm for identity security.

Topics not addressed

As mentioned above, frameworks and regulations simply don't address many desirable features and practices and say little or nothing about topics like implementation.

Slow development

CSFs and regulatory standards are developed through extensive collaboration among industry and government entities. This process, while thorough, is inherently slow and usually lags behind the swift pace of threat actors with their technological advancements in AI, social engineering, and other techniques and tools. Consequently, organizations relying on guidelines developed by committees often find themselves implementing outdated measures or neglecting newer solutions capable of countering current cyber threats.

Similarly, insurance providers are now incorporating more detailed requirements (which draw heavily on existing CSFs) but are still coming up the learning curve. They enforce the use of important fundamental controls, but rarely the adoption of emerging solutions and best practices.

Cloud and AI innovation

Finally, rapid innovation in the realm of AI and by cloud service providers has outpaced the evolution of CSFs. Organizations must be sure they are appropriately applying foundational security principles in fast-changing public cloud, SaaS, and AI environments.

The bottom line on CSFs, standards, and insurance

Organizations should treat CSFs, regulatory standards, and insurance requirements as minimum (albeit mandatory) baselines, not as ceilings or ultimate goals. Forward-thinking organizations must stay agile by continuously updating their identity security strategies to include the latest threat intelligence and technological advancements as well as evolving regulatory mandates.

Takeaways and recommendations

- CSFs provide foundational guidelines and controls that help organizations protect their information assets. However, they are not exhaustive.

- There is often a lag between current threats and the guidance provided by these frameworks and standards, leaving organizations vulnerable if they rely solely on these sources for security measures.

- Rapid innovation by CSPs has outpaced the evolution of CSFs.

- Insurance underwriting requirements have become more stringent, but still don't address the latest technologies and best practices.

- Organizations must continuously update security strategies with the latest threat intelligence and technological developments.

- To stay ahead of threats and adapt to rapid change, organizations should go beyond industry frameworks and standards and embrace the principles and practices of the new paradigm for identity security.

Chapter 13

Developing Your Identity Security Program

In this chapter

- Understand why identity security is the cornerstone of a cybersecurity strategy
- Review the 10 questions and four tenets that can help you define and improve your identity security program
- Pick up ideas for using maturity models and roadmaps to guide and track the progress of your program

We know it's hard to ensure your organization is secure from cyber threats. The work you've done thus far has set the baseline for protecting your business. Now it's time to evolve your strategy and programs and take them to the next level... with identity security at the core.

In this chapter, we offer actionable guidance and best practices to evolve and manage your own identity security program.

Identity Security Is the Cornerstone of a Cybersecurity Strategy

Once, we could think of security as a strong fence and a locked gate. Anyone inside the fence could be trusted to move around freely.

Today, threat actors not only rattle the locks on the gate, they also scrutinize every device, system, and person inside the house. Each object, human and non-human alike, has an identity that, if compromised, is a possible point of entry to gain unauthorized access, steal sensitive information, and disrupt operations.

Because identity is central to a high percentage of recent breaches, it's imperative to position identity security as a primary focus of your security strategy. In fact, because so many security domains depend on trustworthy identities, we can say that identity security is the cornerstone of a robust security strategy.

Hype? We think not.

Is it hype to compare identity security to a cornerstone?

If you remove a cornerstone from a stone wall, the wall will probably crack or even collapse. If threat actors capture identities and valid credentials, the security controls that rely on them are likely to fail. This includes controls for authentication, authorization, access control, data protection, network security, endpoint security, and governance.

That's why we believe the cornerstone analogy is rock-solid.

The primary protective control

Identity security must be viewed as the primary protective control, aligning with the NIST Cybersecurity Framework (CSF) 2.0, where "protect" precedes "detect" and "respond." This proactive stance is vital as detection and response mechanisms heavily rely on identity security. A compromised identity—human or machine—can navigate through an organization and pose significant risks. Staying ahead of the latest identity attacks necessitates being on the cutting edge of identity security practices, ensuring comprehensive protection in today's rapidly evolving threat landscape. (see Figure 13-1).

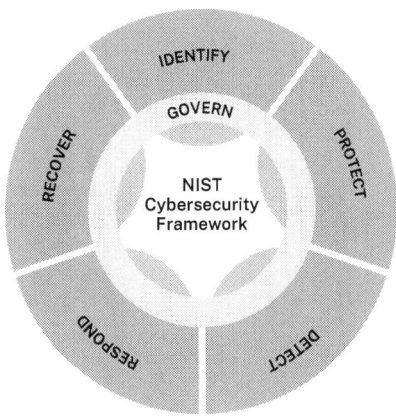

Figure 13-1: Overview of the NIST Cybersecurity Framework 2.0.

A prerequisite for zero trust and compliance

It is also fair to say that strong identity security is a prerequisite for zero trust and compliance.

Identity security is the key to an effective zero trust initiative. In a zero trust architecture, no users are implicitly trusted and requests to access resources are continuously assessed. But when identities are compromised, threat actors can undermine the authentication and authorization processes at the heart of zero trust implementations.

Ten Questions to Guide Your Identity Security Program

Before transforming your current identity security program, it is important to obtain an accurate snapshot of your organization's drivers, goals, and current state. The information you gather will help you make better decisions about how to build the next phases of your program.

Here are 10 questions to help determine areas of focus for your identity security journey:

1. What audit, compliance, regulatory, and cyber insurance requirements do we have?

2. Where can we improve operational efficiencies in supporting our protected identities and users?

3. How can we enable our business by ensuring the security of interactions with cloud service platforms and SaaS services?

4. Are we in the middle of any mergers or acquisitions that require us to secure new environments?

5. Are we getting enough value from our current identity security investments, and are there opportunities to better integrate our tech stack and reduce the number of our identity security vendors?

6. What current and emerging attacks and threats should be our biggest focus areas?

7. What insider threats do we need to mitigate?

8. What identity-related remediation activities do we need to improve?

9. Are there high-priority projects sponsored by executives that we need to consider, for example, implementing a zero trust framework?

10. Which identities and enterprise resources are we protecting today, with what controls, and which ones are unprotected or inadequately protected?

 A good starting point is to cross-reference your existing IAM, PAM, and DevOps standards and security policies with your inventory reports. This will help you understand your landscape more accurately, avoid assumptions, and focus your identity security efforts more effectively.

Four Tenets to Operationalize Identity Security

We'd like to suggest four tenets to help implement an advanced identity security program. They will help you operationalize key concepts such as continuous delivery and execution and the use of clearly defined roles and responsibilities.

Cradle-to-grave identity lifecycle management and governance

A security-first approach to the classic joiner, mover, leaver, and governance processes requires that from the moment a new identity is created it's automatically protected with the appropriate intelligent privilege controls.

Human identities: When your human resources information system (HRIS) onboards or offboards a person, access controls should be applied based on their defined role or function in the organization (i.e., RBAC should be used). This process should extend to granting appropriate access to workforce applications via SCIM/API provisioning (outbound provisioning) and granting access to privileged resources via the relevant intelligent privilege control services and access policy.

Automatic identity governance certification campaigns should be run on a recurring basis against high-risk SaaS applications, cloud environments, elastic cloud workloads, and long-lived systems. Access to enterprise resources should be revoked when users change roles or responsibilities and no longer require it.

Machine identities: Anytime a developer or application owner instantiates a new workload that requires secrets, their request to create a new machine identity should coincide with automated onboarding of the machine identity to the appropriate secrets management service.

Conversely, any time a workload is decommissioned, its access should be revoked automatically and the machine identity terminated.

Enforcement of security at inception

From the moment they're created, new enterprise resources and privileged access to them should be protected with appropriate intelligent privilege controls. To make this process scalable, you need automation and orchestration services.

For example, by using services like Terraform or Ansible to provision new enterprise resources such as CSP accounts, elastic cloud resources, and long-lived systems, organizations can tap into existing automated playbooks and instruction files that provide identity security controls needed by the new resources.

In addition:

☑ New CSP accounts should enable human access to cloud-native services and secrets management for cloud-native workloads.

☑ New elastic cloud workloads and long-lived systems should permit federated human access.

☑ Self-service access requests for privileged access to existing systems should be assessed and granted automatically through similar automated processes.

Following this approach can ensure that organizations will adopt and maintain a proactive security posture.

Ongoing discovery

While proactively protecting resources at inception is vital to long-term success, your organization must also account for the identification and capture of identities and privileged access created outside of standard security processes.

It would be naïve to assume that no identity, account or resource will ever be created outside of approved processes. To address edge cases and previously unknown accounts, identity security teams should implement ongoing discovery across the full spectrum of identities.

RACI matrices

In project management, RACI matrices define the roles and responsibilities of project team members (RACI stands for **Responsible, Accountable, Consulted, Informed**). A RACI matrix makes visible the relationship between roles and tasks.

Teams that create a RACI matrix can reduce or avoid inefficient processes, internal service disruptions, functional delays, and poor internal customer and user experiences.

Figure 13-2 provides a simplified view of a RACI matrix for security teams to use in operationalizing their identity security program.

	Program Director	Operations / Automation	Engineering	End-User
Submit Privileged Access Request	I	A	C	R
Onboard Privileged Access	A	R	C	I
Configure New Security Policy	A	C	R	I
Manage Production Environment	A	C	R	I

Figure 13-2: Simplified view of a RACI matrix for an identity security team.

ON THE WEB

As you develop a RACI matrix, ask yourself: *what standard operating procedures, functions, and activities comprise our program or initiative?* For more information on how to build an identity security RACI matrix, go to the "Defined RACI matrix to support processes" section of the CyberArk Blueprint operationalize web page (https://docs.cyberark.com/cyberark-blueprint/latest/en/content/operationalize-identity-security.htm#RACI).

Metrics and Reporting

Identity security teams do critical work safeguarding corporate and customer data. Good metrics and reporting enable them to articulate the value of this work to cybersecurity leaders and achieve alignment between operational teams and management. Metrics aren't just numbers; they contain narratives that help stakeholders, from program managers to CISOs, understand, measure, and enhance their organization's security posture.

Customize metrics for each audience

Effective cybersecurity programs categorize metrics and KPIs in a hierarchical structure, designed to meet the needs of various audiences within the organization. At higher levels, the metrics become more condensed and strategic:

1. Program managers require detailed, granular metrics that offer rich insights into various aspects of identity security.

2. Directors and vice presidents need metrics that provide wider insights into overall performance and risks.

3. CISOs will be most engaged by curated lists of metrics that summarize critical aspects of identity security to inform strategic decisions and board-level discussions.

4. Board members prefer high-level metrics clearly tied to business risks and opportunities for the organization.

Define metrics by identity security area

Key metrics typically span six major identity security areas:

☑ Access management

☑ Lifecycle management

☑ Privileged access management

☑ Secrets management

☑ Endpoint identity security

☑ ITDR

For each category, organizations should define risk mitigation metrics (e.g., the percentage of identities, processes, accounts, and controls covered), and duration metrics (e.g., the average time it takes to perform key security tasks). Insights from these metrics inform security leaders about the overall state of identity security across the organization.

These metrics help organizations answer the question, "How am I doing compared to my target?" These key performance indicators (KPIs) should align to specific objective key results (OKRs), which should be defined with your security team leadership and mapped to your program roadmap. Organizational objectives are what security leaders consider trying to accomplish, with key results related to the milestones for the objective. For example, if the objective is to protect all IT user access to enterprise systems across the entire organization, security leaders may use several different KPIs to inform how they are progressing to that goal.

CISOs should insist on regular updates from their reports on key metrics to ensure continuous improvement and accountability.

Vice presidents and directors should work collaboratively to define metrics that accurately measure their program's efforts. These metrics should align to specific KPIs and milestones that appear in the roadmap for the identity security program (discussed below).

Track Program Progress with a Maturity Model

Maturity models help security leaders assess the strength of their IT programs relative to those of peer organizations. Most models use a structured approach with four or five maturity levels that represent progressively higher degrees of process capability. Each maturity level includes a collection of related best practices that help organizations achieve specific goals for process improvement.

By reviewing maturity levels, identity security leaders can assess their current level of status in a qualitative way, and learn about tools, techniques, and steps to advance their program to the next level. A maturity model also provides an objective yardstick that technical and non-technical managers can use to track the progress of their identity security program.

The figure below illustrates the value of a maturity model by briefly reviewing the levels in CyberArk's identity security program process maturity model, which is based on the ISACA Capability Maturity Model Integration (CMMI) (see Figure 13-3).

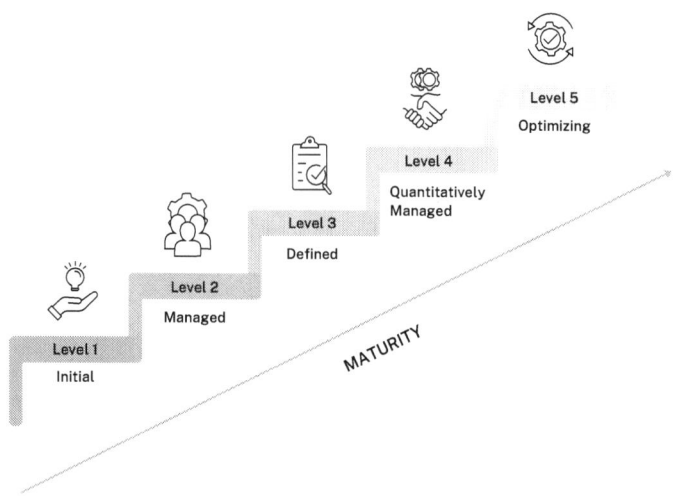

Figure 13-3: Overview of the ISACA Capability Maturity Model Integration (MCCI).

Level 1: Initial

At the initial level, an organization may not have a defined process for managing privileged access. It may have an ad hoc process that is unpredictable, poorly controlled, and reactive. Further, its identity security program may rely on manual processes, spreadsheets, or other inefficient methods. There may be a lack of visibility into which users have privileged access and what actions they are taking.

Level 2: Managed

At the managed level, an organization has established basic processes for managing privileged access. It may have implemented an identity security solution with centralized management and control over privileged access. This solution might include defined roles and responsibilities for managing privileged access and a process for discovering, onboarding, requesting, approving, and auditing privileged access.

At this level, privileged access management tends to be reactive, with privileged access secured on a project-by-project basis for a subset of identities or resources. Improvements are typically driven by audit findings, penetration tests, or security breaches rather than risk assessments and considered planning. The organization is still operating identity security as a project, not a program.

Level 3: Defined

At this level, an organization's identity security initiative has evolved from project to program. An identity security team has documented processes for managing privileged access and established a standard procedure for discovering, onboarding, requesting, approving, auditing, and governing privileged access.

The program may have defined metrics for measuring the effectiveness of its identity security controls and a process for continuous improvement. It has likely established some level of enterprise-wide standards and policies for privileged access, including well-defined definitions and policy exceptions. It probably has developed an identity security management roadmap with a long-term vision for enhancing the identity security program.

Level 4: Quantitatively Managed

At this level, the identity security program team uses data and metrics to measure the effectiveness of its processes and controls. It may use tools to monitor privileged access to detect anomalies and unauthorized activity. It may also conduct regular audits of privileged access and use the results to improve identity security controls. The organization can quantify the scope of privilege and leverage metrics to establish reportable KPIs about the effectiveness of the identity security program.

Level 5: Optimizing

At the highest level of the model, an organization continuously improves its identity security controls based on data and feedback. The program may use machine learning or other advanced technologies to detect and respond to privileged access risks. The identity security team may also collaborate with other teams within the organization to integrate identity security controls into other processes and systems.

Organizations achieving this level are on the cutting edge of identity security. They are capable of keeping up with identity growth and continuously improving.

Building an Identity Security Roadmap

A program roadmap is a planning document that lays out an implementation path and a phased, risk-based approach, broken down into major workstreams and milestones. It's a foundational guide that allows an organization to act on a specific plan, establish a baseline to report against, and keep the business informed about how things are going.

The impact of organizational bandwidth

A common limiting factor in determining the duration and scope of a roadmap is organizational bandwidth. Planners need to answer questions like:

- ☑ Can multiple teams share responsibilities across different security controls and workstreams?
- ☑ How much can each team accomplish in one period?
- ☑ Can work be delegated to different business units?

The larger the scope of a new capability on the roadmap, the more time is required and the more important it is to assess the priority based on expected ROI. For example, a small, highly targeted plan for short-term remediation may last a few months, while a medium-term multi-technology initiative that replaces manual processes with automated ones might easily take a year.

Avoiding Common Roadblocks

A few common roadblocks cause programs to stutter or stall. The following list explains how to prevent them from stopping progress.

Lack of executive support

Lack of executive support typically results in stalled initiatives and struggles to obtain buy-in from the non-technical line of business managers. To gain executive buy-in, identity security teams should invest time in creating strong business cases and aligning their work to the organization's business initiatives.

Lack of a risk mitigation strategy

Every organization needs a strategy and a plan for reducing risk. Often, the fastest approach, and the one that wins the most credibility, is to build on an existing security or industry framework, industry research, or an analysis of the threat landscape.

Lack of enterprise security policies and standards

Without an enforcement mechanism, identity security teams sometimes fail to persuade business units to protect themselves. A team should solidify executive support and gain consensus on a risk mitigation strategy, then propose an organization-wide control standard.

Take the Next Step

The groundwork you've laid will continue to be a critical component of an advanced information security program. However, we're facing new challenges that require a paradigm shift in how security leaders and practitioners think about identity security. The time to adopt identity security as the cornerstone of your cybersecurity program is now.

Takeaways and recommendations

- Identity security is a prerequisite for zero trust frameworks. Compromised identities can undermine all other security controls, making identity security critical to preventing breaches.

- Maturity models and structured roadmaps can help measure progress, prioritize initiatives based on ROI, and align efforts with organizational goals.

- Customized metrics provide actionable insights to measure performance, mitigate risks, and align security objectives with business goals.

- To prevent stalled initiatives, CISOs must secure executive support, define enterprise-wide security policies, and adopt risk mitigation strategies based on established frameworks or threat landscape analyses. Building a strong business case is essential for success.

Chapter 14

Case Studies

In this chapter

■ Learn from the experiences of other organizations, including Pacific Dental, Healthfirst, Cisco, Carnival, SAP, and Aflac.

dentity security doesn't sit in organizational silos; it is a cooperative effort. In this chapter, we'll show you how other companies collaborated with CyberArk to realize their goals and secure identities throughout their organization. A strong partnership helps security leaders achieve their business outcomes and safeguard their businesses for the future.

Secure Access to Clinical Resources in the Cloud

Pacific Dental Services, one of the largest dental support organizations in the United States, supports 900 offices across 25 states. It partnered with CyberArk to address misconfigurations, unmanaged privileged accounts, and inefficient password management.

"Everyone talks about hackers, breaches, and other cyber threats," shared Nemi George, VP & CISO of Information Security at Pacific Dental Services. "But when you strip it down, most incidents start with you doing things wrong. I read recently that 82 percent of all cybersecurity incidents result from misconfigurations. In the middle of the night, what eats away at me is ransomware. I work in healthcare, and the impact would be severe."

With the CyberArk Identity Security Platform, PDS was able to monitor sessions and safely store, rotate, and isolate credentials for both human and non-human users, secure privileged accounts at scale, centralize its security processes, and implement just-in-time access for tasks. This reduced the risk of lateral attacks by cybercriminals who could otherwise tunnel in using admin rights sitting on devices or passwords stored on countless spreadsheets.

By eliminating manual password management and streamlining access through the CyberArk platform's integration with Okta for single sign-on, PDS didn't just tighten operational efficiency—it also boosted user satisfaction.

Employee feedback highlighted ease of use and productivity enhancements, such as less downtime when accessing clinical resources, which allowed providers to spend more time on patient care.

"CyberArk makes the overall patient experience better, and that is a high priority," George says. "When patients walk into one of our supported practices, they are not left waiting and worrying whether their dental insurance premiums will be paid."

PDS now securely manages 20,000 provider website credentials and secures 5,000 laptops and mobile devices, enabling stronger protection of sensitive patient data, better HIPAA compliance, and a frictionless experience for 14,000 team members.

Demonstrating strong privilege management also helped PDS secure more affordable insurance premiums.

"We joke about it in the industry when we say 'data is the new oil' in healthcare," says George. "Using the tools we get from CyberArk, we're able to identify who's coming in, what they're doing, limit and revoke permissions, and enforce our security policies. Identity is the new firewall. It's the new perimeter, it's the new frontier, it's the new everything. It's a very ingrained part of our security and identity framework and strategy here."

A Unified Platform to Cut Complexity and Cost

Healthfirst, New York's largest not-for-profit health insurer, was facing rapid growth and a burgeoning remote workforce. Brian Miller, CISO of Healthfirst, needed to integrate solutions and eliminate redundant tools that were performing similar functions across their privileged access management and identity protection infrastructure.

Healthfirst chose the CyberArk Identity Security Platform to enable fast and secure privileged access for vendors, consultants, and other authorized external third parties, and to protect secrets, keys, certificates, and authentication data across different environments and cloud platforms. By integrating privileged access and identity protection into a cohesive system, Healthfirst fortified defenses around sensitive health data while also controlling costs.

"One of the things Healthfirst was very excited about was the ability to federate," he says. "With other systems, we were spending lots of dollars on licenses to allow call centers to access our systems. With CyberArk, we were able to federate with their identities and cut costs and licensing fees."

Using CyberArk Identity Security for SSO and adaptive MFA also helped Healthfirst move closer to a zero trust security model and enhance call center access. By centralizing identity controls on a unified platform, the company not only protected the personal health information of 1.8 million members but also provided strong security across 10,000 endpoints—70% of which are remote.

"Everybody talks about zero trust," says Miller. "Zero trust is all about identity. If you can't identify it, stop it, control it, you don't have zero trust. Identity really is the first and last line of defense. If you control identity, then you control every part of the environment. That is why we use CyberArk. This is what helps me sleep at night."

Connecting and Protecting Human and Non-human Identities

Cisco, a multinational digital communications technology giant operating in 180 countries, turned to the CyberArk Identity Security Platform to address security gaps for 50,000 privileged accounts and its vast DevOps pipeline. Before adopting the CyberArk platform, Cisco faced challenges in monitoring privileged user sessions, managing secrets across hybrid and multi-cloud environments, and ensuring security for both human and non-human identities.

"Identity includes multiple types of credentials, permissions, laptops or whatever other device we use for work," says Santosh Prusty, Senior Leader, Enterprise Security Team at Cisco. "The attack surface is vast. And it is not only people; there are non-human identities that every organization needs to secure, control and manage."

The CyberArk Identity Security Platform helped Cisco streamline privileged access governance and automate secrets management for over 40 million API calls per month. Its integration with tools like Duo for MFA and SailPoint simplified onboarding and identity governance, helped reduce manual processes and enabled secure, one-click access for developers and administrators.

Cisco now isolates and monitors over 25,000 sessions monthly, records more than 1,000 hours of sessions daily, and has replaced hard-coded credentials with seamless API-based secrets management. Onboarding, which previously took weeks, now happens automatically in minutes. These advancements enabled Cisco to reduce its attack surface, meet compliance requirements, and plan for future improvements such as passwordless access and just-in-time privileged access.

"By having everything consolidated into one identity security platform, we are effective from a management and operational perspective for privileged access," says Prusty. "We've been able to provide our admins and developers with a secure and flexible way to connect to their assets."

How The World's Largest Private Cloud Secures Privileged Access

In an era when identity-based attacks are becoming more sophisticated, SAP Enterprise Cloud Services (ECS), the world's largest private cloud provider, took a bold step with a cutting-edge identity security strategy built on the principle of zero standing privileges.

With operations spanning hundreds of thousands of servers and supporting over 6,000 of the world's largest organizations across multiple industries, SAP ECS is critical in enabling businesses to transform into sustainable, intelligent enterprises.

However, attackers are targeting privileged accounts, which can pose significant security risks if not managed effectively. With the CyberArk Identity Security Platform, SAP eliminated always-on access and enforced just-in-time privileges across all cloud consoles, applications, and databases. By integrating multiple capabilities into a single interface, SAP ECS not only reduced vulnerabilities but also simplified auditing processes and aligned with global regulatory standards.

Through its partnership with CyberArk, SAP ECS has implemented a cutting-edge identity security strategy built on the principle of zero standing privileges that safeguards high-risk access points. "The deployment of CyberArk is central to building next-generation identity security for our business and reinforcing the trust of its global customer base," says Roland Costea, CISO of SAP ECS.

An Identity-first Approach to Smooth Sailing

Carnival Corporation, known for delivering memorable vacation experiences aboard its fleet of 95 cruise ships, faces a unique set of cybersecurity challenges.

Each ship functions not only as a "floating hotel" but also as a "floating data center," with limited network connectivity and thousands of employees and guests relying on secure systems. For Carna Hartman, Director of Identity Access Management at Carnival, the stakes are clear: "If we do our job poorly, it's not going to be a lot of fun for our guests. A great way not to have fun is to come home and find out your credit card or personal information has been leaked."

To address these challenges, Carnival partnered with CyberArk to strengthen its identity security and privileged access management capabilities. CyberArk's solutions play a critical role in securing Carnival's IT environment by protecting privileged accounts and ensuring robust access controls.

"CyberArk holds the keys to the kingdom," Hartman explains. "As we log in each morning, CyberArk is one of the tools in our belt that helps ensure everything is secure." The CyberArk Identity Security Platform is essential to Carnival's identity-first security strategy—preventing attackers from moving laterally within company systems so everyone can have a safe, enjoyable vacation.

The results of this partnership extend beyond technology; they reinforce customer trust. "Everyone thinks of Carnival as having a good time, but for us, identity security is the foundation of everything," Hartman emphasizes. "Every employee, every task ties back to an identity."

Trust Is the Cornerstone of Aflac's Commitment to Customers

Aflac, an insurance leader known for its iconic Aflac Duck mascot, places trust and service at the heart of its operations. With a legacy of providing financial support during life's most challenging moments, Aflac understands the critical importance of protecting its customers' data and its globally recognized brand.

"We sell a promise," says Jay Coull, Senior Manager, Security Administration at Aflac. "Our policyholders put a lot of trust in us, and our promise is that we'll be there for you when you need us." This philosophy extends to their cybersecurity efforts, where they rely on the CyberArk Identity Security Platform to protect sensitive information and enable secure access across the organization.

In a world where traditional security perimeters no longer suffice, CyberArk's identity-first approach has become essential.

Aflac uses the CyberArk Identity Security Platform to monitor and manage both human and machine identities for its vast network of employees and customers while maintaining the speed and efficiency required for modern business. "Identity is the new perimeter," Coull says. "We are no longer in a world where you can build a moat around things. Security needs to be built around the identities."

Aflac trusts CyberArk to manage all of its access. The partnership reflects Aflac's commitment to staying vigilant in an evolving threat landscape and securing not just data but also the trust and reputation that underpin its promise to customers. "They take ownership and help us get to that next level," Jay says.

Achieving a return on your investment

Protecting and managing the vast number of identities across the workforce, IT user, developer, and machine segments are a challenge for any CISO or program director.

As organizations continue to pursue digital transformation, CISOs struggle to communicate the ROI of securing identities to the C-suite and the board of directors, as mentioned in Chapter 12. Understanding the business value of an identity security solution and calculating its ROI will provide you with the data to take on this task.

A recent study by IDC calculated the impact and the business value of implementing CyberArk Identity Security solutions. Findings included:

- A 309% three-year ROI
- A 10-month payback period
- $275,000 in average efficiency benefits and savings per 10 CyberArk protected business applications
- A 49% increase in the efficiency of the IT infrastructure team
- A 35% increase in developer productivity

Measuring the success of your identity security program is a combination of showing ROI and your other program OKRs, as mentioned in our previous chapter. Results also depend on having a solid identity security strategy and program roadmap.

Source: IDC White Paper, sponsored by CyberArk, "The Business Value of CyberArk," IDC #US52652224, November 2024.

IV. Navigating the Future

Chapter 15

The Power of AI

In this chapter

- Learn about the dual role of AI in threats
- Understand how AI can enhance the productivity and effectiveness of identity security teams
- Explore how to ensure AI systems are secure

I n a world where generative artificial intelligence (GenAI) reshapes every aspect of our digital landscape, securing it—and defending against it—have become as crucial as using it. For CISOs, the message is clear: do not rest on your laurels.

Malicious Uses of AI Are Soaring

AI gives attackers an edge. Mere rookies can launch large-scale attacks more efficiently, quickly analyze vast amounts of data to identify vulnerabilities, and make breaches more effective and harder to detect. AI-driven deepfakes and disinformation are also on the rise.

Experts estimate that in 2024, GenAI tools increased vulnerability exploitation by 180% year over year. According to the CyberArk 2024 Identity Security Threat Landscape Report, 90% of organizations experienced a security breach due to phishing or vishing scams and were bracing for more impacts in the next 12 months. The report also found that 75% of executives and employees believe they could tell the difference between a real image and a deepfake created by AI. In reality, these types of campaigns are highly effective at deceiving humans. These threats have given rise to global initiatives to control dangers related to AI like the Artificial Intelligence

Act in the EU and the Executive Order on Promoting the Safe and Ethical Development and Use of Artificial Intelligence Technologies in the United States.

ON THE WEB You can learn more about how threat actors have been using AI in the "Verizon 2024 Data Breach Investigations Report" (https://www.verizon.com/business/resources/reports/dbir/) and the FBI press release, "FBI Warns of Increasing Threat of Cybercriminals Utilizing Artificial Intelligence" (https://www.fbi.gov/contact-us/field-offices/sanfrancisco/news/fbi-warns-of-increasing-threat-of-cyber-criminals-utilizing-artificial-intelligence).

CyberArk Labs researchers were among the first to sound the alarm about GenAI's ability to create highly evasive, polymorphic malware capable of slipping undetected past most security products. They have also seen ChatGPT used to generate persistence techniques, anti-virtual machine modules, and other malicious payloads. They have noted how malware might be used to send requests to ChatGPT through its API and receive back customized malicious code. This scenario presents significant challenges for security professionals and would make mitigation a nightmare.

TECH TALK Want to see how CyberArk Labs used GenAI to create polymorphic malware? Check out "Chatting Our Way Into Creating a Polymorphic Malware" (https://www.cyberark.com/resources/threat-research-blog/chatting-our-way-into-creating-a-polymorphic-malware) or the related podcast "Hacking ChatGPT" (https://share.transistor.fm/s/7cab31ac).

Three Pillars of Security in AI

The future of identity security directly intersects with AI. Its powerful capabilities can revolutionize the way we enhance our security. However, universal standards and best practices for the secure use and development of AI are sorely lacking.

CISOs face three critical directives as they take an AI-first approach to their digital transformation initiatives. They must defend against threats that leverage AI, use AI to enhance their organization's security posture, and secure their AI infrastructure as a whole—including the new identities created by AI applications. Figure 15-1 summarizes key elements of these three pillars for supporting security in a world of AI.

Pillars to Securing AI

Defend Against Threats	Enhance Security Posture	Secure the AI Infrastructure
Establish clear **AI usage guidelines.**	**Adopt AI to rapidly process data** and to predict and prevent threats faster.	**Train AI using secure development code** that follows best practices.
Ensure **comprehensive awareness training** for frontline teams.	**Streamline incident response** through AI-driven automation.	**Enact strict deployment protocols** when transitioning an AI system from testing to operations.
Implement **least privilege** and **assume breach** approaches.	Use AI **to enable policy creation** based on actions and behaviors.	**Protect user data** from theft and jailbreaking.

Figure 15-1: Three pillars for using AI to enhance security.

Pillar 1: Defend Against Threats That Leverage AI

AI plays a dual role in emerging threats because it can both accelerate new threats and enhance old ones. We are seeing a proliferation of new and sophisticated phishing and deepfake campaigns, as well as a reboot of greatest hits like brute-force attacks that can exploit vulnerabilities with unprecedented precision.

As GenAI adoption continues to soar (reaching 99% in some industries), CISOs and other security leaders must work closely with cybersecurity vendors and specialists to ensure their organizations are keeping pace by evolving their security strategies and investing in advanced defensive technologies. AI must be incorporated into identity security controls—and not viewed as replacements for them. It's critical that we:

☑ Enact phishing-resistant MFA mechanisms

☑ Ensure comprehensive awareness training for front-line teams

☑ Limit damage by adhering to least privilege principles, zero standing privileges, and the assumption that organizations will be breached

Pillar 2: Use AI to Enhance Your Security Posture

When organizations explore identity security solutions, they find that systems utilizing AI technologies can help predict and prevent threats with remarkable speed and accuracy. AI can process reams of data and identify anomalies and potential threats in real time. Machine learning (ML) algorithms can also recognize patterns that might be missed by human analysts, enabling faster detection of sophisticated attacks.

Solutions with AI-driven automation can streamline incident response processes by automatically containing threats, analyzing attack vectors, and even initiating countermeasures without human intervention, drastically reducing response times. AI can also be used to analyze trends and historical data, allowing security teams to proactively address gaps before they are exploited.

We may eventually see AI handling access policy creation based on past actions and behaviors, enabling dynamic and personalized access that keeps up with each user's evolving needs, cuts down on repetitive tasks and frees up security professionals to focus on high-priority initiatives.

CAUTION

When you create or modify policies, don't forget to test the effects before moving to production. AI capabilities make this a much easier task, but they don't eliminate the need for testing.

AI in the SOC

SOCs can employ AI to analyze vast amounts of identity-centric threat data in real time and work with security orchestration, automation and response (SOAR) systems to optimize response workflows. Using AI doesn't just reduce the workloads of human analysts, it also exponentially increases analytic capabilities while driving down mean time to detection and mean time to response.

AI systems don't usually work in isolation—they communicate with other technologies like databases, websites, or devices. Their use must be closely managed to ensure they operate within predefined, secure parameters and don't access unauthorized data, behave unpredictably, or break into other connected systems.

Pillar 3: Secure the AI Infrastructure as a Whole

As organizations continue to integrate AI into products and services to increase efficiency, they must proactively secure how these solutions and services are developed, deployed, and used.

Secure Development: AI systems learn from training data (like text, images, or videos) that teaches the technology how to make decisions or solve problems. Developers who write code and create models that help AI systems process this information must follow strong security practices that ensure training data is clean and representative. These safeguards prevent biases and vulnerabilities that can be exploited by attackers.

Secure Deployment: When an AI system is moved from the testing phase to an operational environment where it interacts with users or other systems, security risks abound. Attackers might tamper with the AI system to change how it behaves, gain unauthorized access to the sensitive data the AI processes, or manipulate inputs to trick the AI system.

The operational environment must adhere to strict identity security measures to protect it from tampering, unauthorized access, and manipulation.

Secure Use: It's critical to protect the data that users access and ensure they trust the system and its outputs. Specifically, we need to ensure users' access can't be leveraged by attackers to steal data or perform jailbreaking: bypassing restrictions or safeguards in an AI system to make it provide information it's not intended to handle. This is often done by exploiting weaknesses in the model's design or prompt processing.

While AI-based products—including the internal use of large language models (LLMs)—have huge potential for good, organizations must also implement proactive measures to keep them secure.

You can read more about securing LLMs and why they require extra caution in the next chapter.

AI in action: three scenarios

A financial services firm uses an AI tool to monitor network traffic and detect unusual patterns of access and attempts to reach sensitive customer data. When this tool detects a possible attack, it automatically triggers an alert and isolates the potentially compromised account. It also suggests immediate containment actions to prevent what could be a massive data breach.

A healthcare provider uses an AI-based product to manage access to its patient records systems. The product analyzes access patterns that suggest phishing, such as rapid access attempts from several geographic locations. It then triggers step-up MFA requests and alerts the security team.

An overworked audit team uses an AI solution to analyze and summarize the contents of event logs. It can sum up hours of sessions in 30 seconds, showing what commands were used and what applications were accessed.

Safeguarding the Upcoming Evolution in AI Identities

GenAI is poised to transform its role from a tool that assists humans with content creation and decision-making into a source for fully autonomous agents capable of executing tasks, making independent decisions, and driving organizational changes with or without human supervision and pre-approval.

By 2028, at least 15% of day-to-day work decisions will be made autonomously through agentic AI, up from zero percent in 2024. For enterprises, this shift will represent a seismic leap—and create a sizable struggle.

One of the most pressing challenges will be securing the identities of AI-related entities at scale across diverse systems and geographies. Traditional IAM systems are not equipped to handle the authentication, authorization, and monitoring protocols for thousands or millions of AI agents. New frameworks should include:

- ☑ Controls that ensure AI identities are used appropriately and not exploited for unauthorized access
- ☑ Governance that allows for continuous visibility into the activities of AI-driven identities
- ☑ Codes of conduct that ensure AI aligns with ethical standards and regulatory requirements

As GenAI becomes capable of acting independently, we face big challenges in managing these new digital identities. Putting the right guardrails in place from day one can help maximize the benefits while keeping risks under control.

AI and the Talent Shortage

The cybersecurity industry faces a talent shortage of over four million professionals, and identity security is particularly impacted. Many organizations are turning to GenAI and ML to help bridge these gaps, upskill existing teams, boost productivity through automation, and improve their defensive strategies.

GenAI, ML, and automation technologies can make cybersecurity careers more enticing by eliminating manual drudgery and emphasizing creativity, analytical thinking, and other uniquely human characteristics. For example, an AI system to support endpoint security policy creation might be able to deliver prescriptive recommendations within minutes, rather than requiring hours of sifting through alerts manually and developing policies based on these alerts.

CISOs must invest in people through training, open hiring practices, and tailored development programs. AI and ML can elevate security programs and reinvigorate cybersecurity careers.

ON THE WEB Read more in the blog: "GenAI's Role in Upskilling to Close the Cybersecurity Skills Gap" (https://www.cyberark.com/resources/blog/genais-role-in-upskilling-to-close-the-cybersecurity-skills-gap).

AI, Done Right, Can Transform

Despite all this potential, analysts predict that by 2025, 30% of GenAI projects will fail due to poor planning, unclear goals, or escalating costs. Thoughtful strategy, leadership support, and consistent implementation can unlock its full impact.

CISOs should focus on clear use cases, such as automating document reviews or enhancing customer support, and roll out tools in small, focused phases to build confidence and adoption. How-to videos, webinars, and on-demand learning libraries help employees maximize the potential of new tools.

Leadership buy-in is critical. Managers who champion GenAI, integrate it into workflows, and foster a culture of experimentation see higher adoption rates across teams. Even simple team-building activities—like composing a poem with GenAI—can inspire curiosity and innovation.

Takeaways and recommendations

GenAI can help organizations improve:
- **Threat detection** by analyzing patterns in network traffic and user behavior to detect anomalies that may indicate security threats
- **Access controls** by automatically assessing user activity and risk
- **Incident response** by generating near-real-time incident reports and recommends response actions

To mitigate risk, organizations must:
- **Establish protocols** to authenticate, monitor, and manage new identities like bots
- **Continuously evolve defensive strategies** to counteract AI-powered threats and invest in tools that keep up with evolving AI capabilities
- **Ensure data integrity** and maintain ethical standards with strict security practices governing the AI infrastructure

Chapter 16

LLMs Require Extra Caution

In this chapter

- Discover how LLMs can serve both as transformative tools and as potential threat vectors
- Learn about actionable strategies to prevent exploitation.

arge language models (LLMs) are central to AI. Their ability to process and generate human-like text has unlocked transformative possibilities across industries. However, for CISOs, this potential introduces significant security challenges, as LLMs are highly susceptible to manipulation and must be secured.

The Double-edged Sword of LLMs

When integrated with external software, LLMs are highly versatile systems capable of complex tasks. However, in the wrong hands, their adaptability can transform LLMs from powerful assistants to active threat vectors that can be manipulated to execute database queries, run external API calls, or even access networked machines.

Studies show alarmingly high success rates for attack attempts, such as jailbreaking to bypass safety restrictions or generating harmful outputs. Even innocuous interactions with LLMs can be manipulated to trigger arbitrary code execution, underscoring the real-world implications. CISOs must implement robust security frameworks—rather than just system prompts or alignment strategies.

A Call to Action for CISOs

As LLMs integrate into workflows involving human, machine, and AI-generated identities, their vulnerabilities must be addressed to safeguard these ecosystems. Adopting principles like ZSP ensures that LLMs operate with just-in-time access and minimal permissions, mitigating identity exploitation.

To reduce risks in LLM integrations, CISOs must:

☑ **Never rely on LLMs as security boundaries.** Limit the abilities you give them and don't trust alignment prompts to enforce security.

☑ **Follow the principle of least privilege (PoLP).** Give LLMs the minimum access needed to perform tasks.

☑ **Sanitize LLM output.** Always validate output to remove any potentially harmful content, such as XSS payloads.

☑ **Sandbox LLMs when necessary.** Isolate them to prevent malicious code execution.

☑ **Sanitize training data.** Ensure attackers can't exploit sensitive information through training data.

ON THE WEB Learn how CyberArk Labs devised ways to jailbreak LLMs and render them resistant to adversarial attacks. Read: "Operation Grandma: A Tale of LLM Chatbot Vulnerability" (https://www.cyberark.com/resources/threat-research-blog/operation-grandma-a-tale-of-llm-chatbot-vulnerability).

Takeaways and recommendations

- LLMs offer transformative potential but can be exploited to execute harmful actions. Security frameworks are essential.

- Applying principles like least privilege, sandboxing, and output sanitization is key to protecting identity ecosystems.

Chapter 17

Quantum Readiness

In this chapter

- Be introduced to quantum computing and its impact on identity systems.
- See why identity security is critical for addressing this exceptional threat
- Explore a phased approach to quantum readiness

Even as we're exploring the transformative potential of generative AI and LLMs, we're also on the brink of another seismic technological event. Quantum computing, which leverages quantum phenomena to perform calculations such as those used in cryptanalysis exponentially faster than conventional computing, is coming fast. While it promises exciting advancements, it's also throwing down the gauntlet and threatening the foundation of cybersecurity: identity.

Mankind's Best/Worst Breakthrough

Quantum computers can process vast amounts of data at unprecedented speeds. While today's binary computers can complete a puzzle piece by piece, quantum computers can simultaneously look at and solve for all the possibilities. Qubits, the fundamental particle units of quantum computers, represent multiple states at once and affect each other instantly, regardless of the distance between them.

Such unparalleled processing power promises breakthroughs in medicine, climate modeling, and beyond, heralding revolutionary advancements for humanity. Unfortunately, quantum computers and methods like Shor's Algorithm could potentially break public key cryptography like Rivest-Shamir-Adleman (RSA). This milestone would affect not only private communications but also the entire identity system for human and machine authentication and authorization.

ON THE WEB Want to do a deeper dive into post-quantum cryptography? Read: "Quantum Computing is Going to Kill Classic Cryptography. But We Can Still Save It" (https://medium.com/cyberark-engineering/quantum-computing-is-going-to-kill-classic-cryptography-but-we-can-still-save-it-6973e64b89c3).

The problem? Adjusting to quantum computing's challenges to all things digital will not be a one-day task, but instead will play out over many years. Post-quantum attacks will first be developed by nation-states, and over time will become available to many other potential attackers.

The disruptive potential extends beyond encryption of data at rest; it will fundamentally reshape how we think about identity security.

The Quantum Threat to Identity Systems

Identity security for humans and machines is built on asymmetric cryptography that has been in use for 50 years. Unfortunately, quantum attacks might be able to successfully impersonate human and machine identities and overcome foundational identity security technologies, from TLS certificates, to access tokens, to secured vaults, to code signing.

Encryption algorithms used within identity security control planes will become vulnerable to quantum cracking. Risks could include compromising the integrity of SAML assertions and protocols such as RDP over TLS. Attackers leveraging quantum computing may be able to bypass these security measures and compromise the very backbone of identity security.

The threat is already here. Any data or encrypted authentication material stolen by threat actors now can be saved and decrypted later. Nation-state actors are believed to already be collecting encrypted communications and data, positioning themselves to exploit it once quantum decryption becomes feasible. Boards of directors and auditors are already beginning to ask questions. Fortunately, this shift will take years to implement and deploy. To protect yourself, now is the time to start preparing.

The Quantum Readiness Journey

To future-proof identity security, organizations must adapt quickly by reevaluating their encryption mechanisms and overall identity security strategy.

Quantum-safe algorithms are here, and applications are being updated. Security and identity teams won't be required to implement new cryptography themselves, but will need to employ identity systems that use the new methods.

Here's a practical roadmap for navigating the journey to quantum readiness and ensuring your identity security strategy remains resilient to quantum threats.

Assess your current state

Take the first steps to evaluate your risk readiness:

- ☑ **Discover all your identities:** This activity extends beyond just encryption mechanisms. Inventory all human and machine identities across your organization, including their cryptographic authentication material like TLS certificates, SSH keys, and code signing certificates. Understand how authentication and access tokens are generated and secured. Identify all vaults and credential stores.

- ☑ **Evaluate risk and conduct triage of critical systems:** Focus on systems that handle mission-critical tasks, sensitive data or operations, as they'll need the highest level of protection.

Get familiar with post-quantum cryptography (PQC)

It's important to understand the algorithms being developed to withstand quantum threats and how these new cryptographic methods can fit into your current systems.

To learn more about how encryption works (and why PQC is so important) tune into Episode 24 of the Trust Issues podcast, "Making the Leap to Post-Quantum Computing Encryption" (https://share.transistor.fm/s/3ac108e4).

Plan for a phased transition

Quantum readiness isn't a "rip and replace" process—it's a gradual migration that requires a clear and deliberate strategy, as follows:

- ☑ **Prioritize high-risk systems:** Focus on the authentication material, such as passwords, certificates, and keys, protecting your most critical infrastructure.

- ☑ **Establish timelines:** A strong business case goes a long way in advancing quantum readiness and avoiding unnecessary disruptions. Consider aligning cryptographic updates with major initiatives (zero trust, cloud computing, passwordless) or use opportunistic timing such as certificate expiration dates.

- ☑ **Create redundancy:** Be sure you have fallbacks during the transition to prevent downtime or vulnerabilities.

Assess infrastructure compatibility

- ☑ **Review your systems** for compatibility with quantum-resistant algorithms.

- ☑ **Identify any upgrades** or adjustments needed to integrate PQC seamlessly.

- ☑ **Check your software vendors** to ensure they're supporting PQC-ready algorithms.

Implement quantum-resistant measures

Once your plan is in place, it's time to roll out quantum-safe solutions across your organization. Here are the key benchmarks:

☑ Ensure every human and machine identity is protected by strong **privilege controls** with **end-to-end lifecycle management.** This protection will enable seamless adoption of quantum-safe algorithms when they are ready.

☑ Transition to upgraded, **quantum-resistant certificates** as they become available.

☑ Implement **passwordless authentication** for human identities to reduce the footprint of PQC-vulnerable authentication material.

☑ **Automate any authentication** material issuance, renewal, and rotation to reduce human error and ensure consistency.

☑ Use **quantum-resistant cryptography** for code signing to protect against tampering. Ensure all signing keys are securely managed and only accessible to authorized users.

☑ Deploy **quantum-safe cryptographic keys** for workload identities, such as containers or virtual machines.

☑ **Monitor and secure all identities** to prevent misuse or exploitation.

☑ **Automate provisioning** processes to streamline deployments and minimize risk.

☑ Monitor to **ensure that changes are implemented** and maintained.

☑ Continuously **check for vulnerabilities** or unusual activity across all machine identities.

Preparation for the Quantum Leap Starts Now

Quantum computing is poised to unlock incredible opportunities—but only if we lay the groundwork. The revolution is already happening in labs and pilot programs around the world. Waiting until quantum computing becomes mainstream to address security challenges is not an option. Organizations must act now to ensure they're ready.

The good news is that investing in identity security is also investing in quantum readiness. From automating TLS certificates to implementing passwordless authentication, identity security initiatives have positive business impacts today that will help you move closer to post-quantum readiness tomorrow.

Takeaways and recommendations

- Quantum computing's ability to break traditional encryption poses a direct threat to identity systems for both human and machine authentication.

- CISOs must begin assessing risks, inventorying identities, and planning phased transitions to quantum-safe cryptographic methods.

- Identity security with privilege controls and quantum-safe encryption will help safeguard identities and systems from post-quantum attacks.

Conclusion

Bad actors have a head start on us; they think aggressively and move fast. To succeed, we must be proactive, move away from a project mindset, and formalize a dynamic approach that helps ensure the *right people* (and machines) get the *right access* to the *right resources* based on the *right policies* and the *right assessments* of risk at the *right moment*. Success in these areas will lead to improved business resilience, higher productivity, and the ability to deploy innovative new technologies and processes more quickly and confidently.

We hope you'll combine the insights and expertise provided in this book with the strategies of security leaders who are redefining identity security alongside you. CyberArk is here to be your trusted partner during this paradigm shift and guide you on your identity security journey.

Securing your identities today lays the foundation for blocking attackers now and in the future from breaching your organization. It will become your competitive advantage and key to business resilience in the future. Together, we'll outpace the threats, disrupt the status quo, and lead the charge in securing the world against cyber threats.